The Pennsylvania Railroad
Under Wire

WILLIAM D. MIDDLETON

D1607305

Kalmbach
BOOKS

Printed in the United States of America

02 03 04 05 06 07 08 09 10 11   10 9 8 7 6 5 4 3 2 1

Visit our website at
http://kalmbachbooks.com
Secure online ordering available

Publisher's Cataloging-in-Publication
(Provided by Quality Books, Inc.)

Middleton, William D., 1928-
    The Pennsylvania Railroad under wire / William D.
Middleton. — 1st ed.
    p. cm. — (Classic trains)
    Includes index.
    ISBN 0-89024-617-3

    1. Pennsylvania Railroad—History. 2. Railroads—
United States—History. I. Title.

TF25.P4M54 2002   385'.0973
                 QBI02-200522

Art director: Kristi Ludwig
Book design: Sabine Beaupré
Map: John Signor

On the cover: In addition to its New York-Washington mainline electrification, the Pennsylvania erected 11,000-volt A.C. catenary over a portion of the New York & Long Branch line that carried heavy traffic to the New Jersey shore. Bound from New York to Bay Head Junction on the coast, a first section of train 787 left the main line at Rahway, N.J., for the New York & Long Branch on a sunny June afternoon in 1947. Heading the long train of P70 coaches was GG1 4901, which would turn the train over to steam power at South Amboy. Arthur F. Knauer photo

Contents

The Pennsylvania Railroad

In the beginning, the Pennsylvania Railroad was an east-west railroad that had been developed largely to strengthen Philadelphia and its port in the competition for trade with the American interior. Early in the nineteenth century, construction of the Erie Canal had given New York a strong advantage in this trade, while Baltimore had gained similar advantage through the construction of the National Road and—later—the building of the pioneer Baltimore & Ohio.

Pennsylvania's initial response to this competition was to begin the development of a system of canals that—with the aid of a 4-mile tunnel under the Alleghenies—would link Philadelphia with Pittsburgh. While a canal between the Schuylkill and Susquehanna Rivers was completed in 1827, the scheme was soon given up as impractical. A new plan called the Main Line of Public Works was chartered in 1828. This was a combination of railroads and canals, with a railroad from Philadelphia to Columbia, on the Susquehanna River, and another across the Allegheny Mountains, with canals from Columbia and Pittsburgh to the base of the mountains on either side. The two canals were completed by 1832, while the Philadelphia-Columbia railroad and the unique Allegheny Portage Railroad over the mountains were ready for business two years later.

This arrangement worked well enough for several years, but when the Baltimore & Ohio set out to link Baltimore with Pittsburgh, Pennsylvania decided that an all-rail route was needed between Philadelphia and Pittsburgh, and the Pennsylvania Railroad was chartered in 1846 to build from Harrisburg to Pittsburgh. Construction began in 1847, and by 1852 the PRR had completed lines that linked Harrisburg and Pittsburgh with the portage railroad, while the Main Line route between Philadelphia and Columbia and a Harrisburg-Lancaster railroad completed an all-rail route

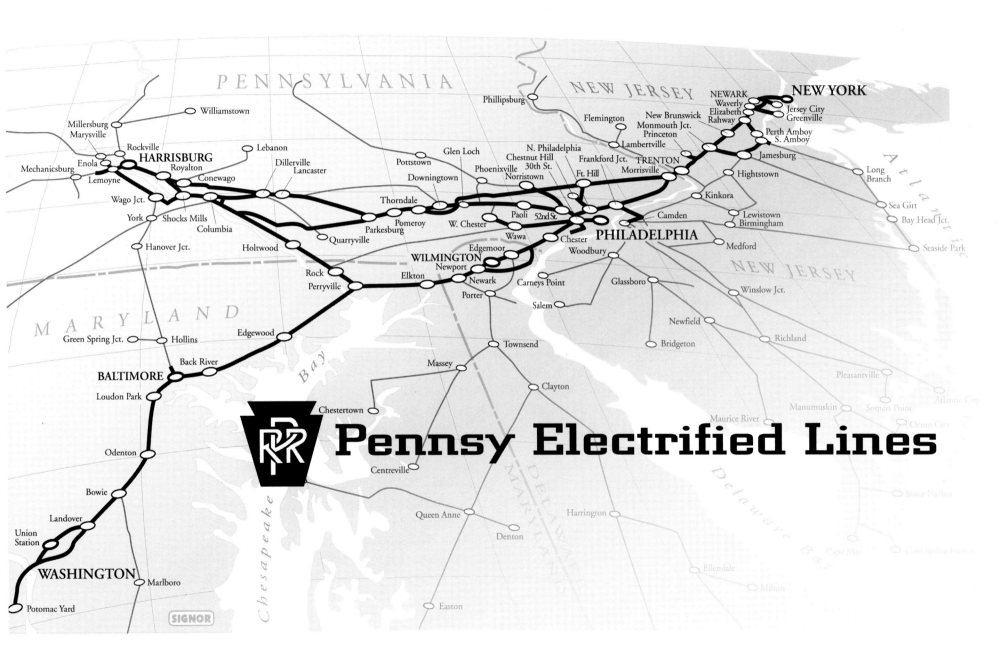

Pennsy Electrified Lines

between the two major Pennsylvania cities. Completion of a line over the Alleghenies and a summit tunnel enabled the Pennsylvania to bypass the portage railroad by 1854, and within the next few years the Pennsylvania acquired or leased its connections east of Harrisburg to establish an all-PRR route across the state. By 1869, through the lease of lines west of Pittsburgh, the Pennsylvania had grown into a system of more than 3000 miles of line that reached all the way to Chicago, St. Louis, and other important points in the Middle West.

Despite all of the state's efforts to strengthen Philadelphia as a major commercial center and port, however, New York had long since become the nation's largest city and its preeminent commercial center, and the Pennsylvania determined that it must have a link of its own to the city. This was achieved in 1871 through lease of the Philadelphia & Trenton and the United Canal & Railroad Companies of New Jersey, which gave the Pennsylvania a route under its own control right to the west bank of the Hudson River at Jersey City, opposite New York City.

At the same time the Pennsylvania looked southward from Philadelphia as well, where the competing B&O was well entrenched. Through control of the Northern Central, the Pennsylvania had gained a route between Harrisburg and Baltimore as early as 1861. The railroad then acquired the charter of the Baltimore & Potomac, a company that had never begun construction, and it completed its planned line to the Potomac, near Pope's Creek, Md., with a branch to Washington, in 1872. The PRR then established through service between its Jersey City terminal and Washington over the Philadelphia, Wilmington & Baltimore, next gaining control of the PW&B in 1881. The major north-south route created by these acquisitions linked the east-west PRR system with the railroads of the south through Washington, and with those of New England through New York City.

As the Northeast's industry flourished and the population grew accordingly in the late nineteenth and early twentieth centuries, these eastern seaboard Pennsylvania main lines grew into some of the most intensively utilized segments of the entire PRR system. By 1896 virtually the entire route from New York to Philadelphia, and west to Harrisburg, had been expanded to four tracks, and there was at least double track all the way to Washington. As freight and passenger traffic climbed to still higher levels after the turn of the century, the Pennsylvania, under President Alexander J. Cassatt, made massive investments to expand capacity still further. The entire New York Division was governed by automatic block signals by 1907. Grade separations were built at key junctions. A new low-grade line for freight traffic was built between the Philadelphia area and the new Enola Yard near Harrisburg, while an elevated line was constructed to carry freight traffic around congested yards at Philadelphia.

Despite all of the improvements, the Pennsylvania was hard pressed to handle its growing traffic on these lines with steam power, and the extraordinary capacity demands and operating requirements of the railroad's eastern main lines would make them the site of what would prove to be the most extensive electrification ever undertaken by any North American railroad.

Pioneer Electrification

The Pennsylvania Railroad was among the very first American railroads to experiment with electric operation. The application of electricity to transportation had occupied inventors throughout much of the nineteenth century. A battery-powered locomotive built by Scottish inventor Robert Davidson had been tested on the Edinburgh & Glasgow Railway as early as about 1838. There were similar experiments in the U.S. over the next several decades, most notably a battery locomotive developed by Dr. Charles G. Page that reached a speed of 19 m.p.h. on a test run between Washington and

Bladensburg, Md., on April 29, 1851. Batteries, however, proved to be an unsuitable source of power, and it was not until the 1870s, following the development of practical electrical generators, that real progress was made towards electric transportation.

German electrician and inventor Dr. Ernst Werner von Siemens successfully demonstrated the first generator-powered electric railway at a Berlin exhibition in 1879. Similar experiments by Stephen D. Field, Thomas Edison, and Leo Daft followed over the next few years, and during 1887-88 a young Naval Academy graduate named Frank J. Sprague developed what is generally considered the first

fully successful electric street railway at Richmond, Va. Wholesale electrification of North America's horse-drawn and cable street railway systems followed over the next decade.

The possibilities of this new form of motive power for steam railroad operations were quickly recognized. An electric locomotive had been tested on the New York elevated railroad as early as 1887, and in the same year a small electric locomotive began hauling coal cars at a Pennsylvania colliery. The Baldwin Locomotive Works built an experimental 60-ton, 1000-h.p. electric locomotive for a proposed suburban electrification at Chicago in 1892, and just a year later the brand new General Electric Company turned out its first electric locomotive, a four-wheel, 30-ton machine that was exhibited at the World's Columbian Exposition in Chicago. A much larger double-truck, 35-ton locomotive completed by GE a year later went to work at a Connecticut cotton mill, where it remained in service for 70 years.

These developments were not lost on the Pennsylvania, and late in 1894 the railroad incorporated the Burlington & Mt. Holly Traction Railroad Company to carry out the electrification of a 7-mile New Jersey branch line to test the feasibility of electric operation for other lines on the system. Among the incorporators of the new traction subsidiary was Samuel Rea, then an assistant to the Pennsylvania's president, who would later be one of the key figures in PRR electrification. The Westinghouse Electric & Manufacturing Company won a contract for the electrification, and work began in March 1895. A simple trolley wire overhead system comparable to street or interurban railway practice was installed, and a 300-h.p. steam-powered generating plant was constructed near the Mt. Holly station. The Jackson &

Sharp Company at Wilmington, Del., built three combination baggage and passenger cars for the line. These were wooden cars 43 feet 6 inches over platforms, much smaller than standard PRR coaches. Two of the cars were powered by two 75-h.p. Westinghouse D.C. motors, while one was powered by four 50-h.p. motors. The cars proved capable of pulling standard PRR coaches at speeds of 45 to 60 m.p.h.

An initial test run was made over part of the line early in June, and regular electric operation began on July 22, 1895, when the electric cars replaced steam trains operating over the branch. The new service was a moderate success. Six daily steam round trips were replaced with ten electric round trips, later increased to 18 weekday round trips, and fares were reduced. Although passenger traffic increased, the service never became profitable. When the Mt. Holly generating plant burned in 1901, the Pennsylvania decided not to rebuild it and brought its pioneer electric operation to an end.

Despite the short life of its Burlington & Mt. Holly experiment, the Pennsylvania was not quite finished with branchline electrification. In 1906 the railroad

electrified an 8-mile branch between Dillsburg and Mechanicsburg, Pa., with an overhead 600-volt D.C. trolley wire. Two old wooden combines were fitted with trolley poles, motors, and controls to operate passenger service over the line. While this electrification lasted much longer than the earlier New Jersey trial, remaining in service until 1928, it attracted little attention. By 1906 the Pennsylvania and several other railroads were involved in much bigger electrification projects than an 8-mile branch line in rural Pennsylvania.

▲ Ornately decorated combination baggage-passenger car No. 3 was one of three built for the Pennsylvania's subsidiary Burlington & Mt. Holly Traction Railroad Company by the Jackson & Sharp Company of Wilmington in 1895. The car was capable of pulling a standard PRR coach. Division of Historical and Cultural Affairs, Dover, Del.

Third Rail to Long Island and the Seashore

▶ Distinctive to the Long Island was the railroad's arch-roofed version of the Pennsylvania's MP54 multiple-unit car. One of them headed an eastbound Port Washington line train into the station at Bayside, N.Y., in March 1947. James G. La Vake photo

By the beginning of the twentieth century, the technology of low-voltage D.C. electrification had advanced to a level at which it promised significant benefits for mainline railroad operations. A 600-volt D.C. system had been adopted for the Baltimore & Ohio's pioneer mainline electrification through the Howard Street tunnel at Baltimore, which began successful operation in 1895. The multiple-unit control system developed by Frank J. Sprague in 1897 had been quickly adopted for elevated and subway rapid-transit services. M.U. control made it possible to control an entire train of electric cars from one control point, permitting the economical operation of trains of any length. With its traction motors distributed throughout a train, an M.U. train typically had a better power-to-weight ratio and could accelerate faster than a locomotive-hauled train.

The advantages of M.U. operation with D.C. power were equally applicable to heavy steam railroad suburban and commuter services, and several railroads soon followed the nation's rapid transit systems in the adoption of the new technology. In 1903 the North Shore Railroad in California converted its steam-powered suburban service in Marin County, north of San Francisco, to third-rail D.C. operation with M.U. equipment. The same year the New York Central chose a similar system for a massive electrification of its New York terminal and two principal suburban lines north of New York City that began operation in 1906.

Two Pennsylvania Railroad subsidiaries were also among the early converts to D.C. third-rail operation.

The first of these to begin electrification was the Long Island Rail Road, which had come under PRR control in 1900. There were several reasons for the Pennsylvania's interest in the LIRR. Control of the Long Island gave it access to freight terminal facilities

10

▲ The sturdy Long Island MP54s carried more than just passengers. Heading this LIRR train at an unidentified station was a baggage-mail version of the durable M.U. car. Bill Myers photo

▲ Typical of the intense rush-hour activity on the Long Island is this scene from the 1940s at Sunnyside Yard in Queens. In the foreground, an 11-car train of empty MP54 M.U. cars is outbound from the East River tunnels and Pennsylvania Station, while beyond another train of MP54s heads for Manhattan with a load of commuters. David P. Morgan Library photo

in Brooklyn. Also, the Long Island would afford access to the bridge then being planned to cross the East River at Hell Gate, which would connect with the New York, New Haven & Hartford to provide a link to New England. Important, too, was the substantial commuter traffic carried by the LIRR between Long Island points and terminals in Brooklyn and in Long Island City, across the East River from Manhattan. A new tunnel planned by the Long Island would bring this traffic under the East River into Manhattan from the Flatbush Avenue terminal in Brooklyn. Traffic was sure to grow,

and Long Island to prosper, with this improved link to Manhattan. The specifics of this plan would change over the next two years as the Pennsylvania formulated its plans for a new Manhattan passenger terminal that would serve the needs of both its own trains and those of its Long Island subsidiary. But in any event, the LIRR would enter Manhattan via long East River tunnels, for which electric operation would be imperative.

The Long Island's initial electrification was a part of an extensive program of improvements to its Atlantic Avenue line in Brooklyn. The work included a long tunnel

under Atlantic Avenue and a new underground terminal at Flatbush Avenue. The electrification totaled 38 route-miles extending from Flatbush Avenue east to Belmont Park in Queens, and south from Woodhaven Junction across Jamaica Bay to Rockaway Park and to Valley Stream via Far Rockaway. Reflecting the expectation that LIRR trains would operate across the East River into Manhattan via the New York subway system, technical standards for the electrification were virtually identical to those for New York's new Interborough Rapid Transit subway. Power was distributed by a 650-volt D.C.

◄ En route to Long Beach from New York, a three-car train of MP54s raced eastward west of Lynbrook, N.Y., in May 1970. Babylon and Montauk Branch trains used the two tracks to the right. Fred W. Schneider III photo

"Change at Jamaica," where the railroad's principal lines meet and diverge, has long been a way of life for many Long Island commuters. Here, in a view westward from Hall Tower at the east end of the station, an outbound train of MP54 M.U. cars pulls away from the platforms, while to the left a steam-powered train prepares to depart. Beyond, to the right, a train of the LIRR's newer double-deck M.U. cars, built by the Pennsylvania's Altoona shops, enters the station. David P. Morgan Library photo

third-rail system, and the Long Island's 234 new 51-foot, steel MP41 M.U. cars designed by electrical engineer George Gibbs were virtually identical to the cars that Gibbs had designed for the IRT.

Construction of the electrical installation began in June 1904, and Long Island electric operation began on July 26, 1905. While the planned operation of LIRR trains over the IRT into Manhattan never did materialize, the railroad was able to establish a through service to lower Manhattan in 1907 by means of a connection with the Brooklyn Rapid Transit elevated line and the Williamsburg Bridge.

Improved Long Island service to Manhattan became available with the opening of Penn Station in 1910, and the bridge route was given up in 1917.

LIRR electrification has continued to expand ever since that 1905 start. With the most recent extension of third rail to Ronkonkoma in 1988, LIRR electrified territory reached a total of some 126 route-miles of the railroad's most heavily used lines. Long Island M.U. rolling stock evolved from the short "Gibbs cars" of the initial electrification through MP54 M.U.s similar to those of the parent Pennsylvania and big double-

deck cars to the 100-m.p.h. high-speed Metropolitan cars of the modern LIRR.

The Long Island electrification was followed only a year later by the similar third-rail installation of another PRR subsidiary, the West Jersey & Seashore. Extending between Camden, across the Delaware River from Philadelphia, and Atlantic City, N.J., with a branch to Millville, N.J., this represented the longest steam railroad electrification yet completed in North America, with a total of 75 route-miles and some 150 track-miles of electric operation. While the Pennsylvania

◀◀ Three generations of Long Island M.U. cars made up this Babylon line train near Baldwin on a winter day in January 1957. Heading the train was one of the railroad's durable arch-roofed MP54s, followed by three Pullman-Standard MP70 cars of mid-1950s origin. Bringing up the rear was a double-deck M.U. built by the Pennsylvania's Altoona shops in the late 1940s. Jim Shaughnessy photo

◀ A new era in Long Island commuting began with the delivery of the first Budd-built M-1 Metropolitan M.U. cars in 1968. Outbound from New York's Penn Station, a ten-car train of M-1s approached Woodside station in May 1970. Above the four-track LIRR main line is New York City Transit's Flushing line. William D. Middleton photo

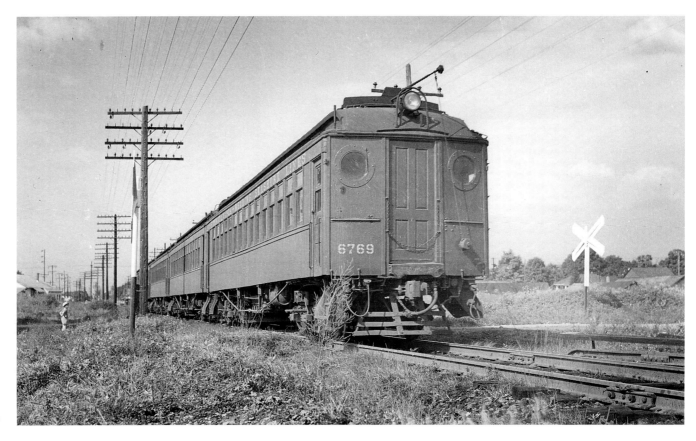

The West Jersey & Seashore's sturdy wooden cars served until almost the very end of electric operation in 1949. Wooden M.U. 6769 headed a Millville-Camden train near Clayton, N.J., in 1947. Porthole end windows and a horizontally barred "hencoop" pilot hinted at the line's PRR origins. David H. Cope photo

The West Jersey & Seashore got a new name in a 1933 merger with the Reading's Atlantic City Railroad. Lettered for the successor Pennsylvania-Reading Seashore Lines, M.U. cars waited between runs at the storage yard near the line's Camden terminal in November 1948. On the right is one of the line's newest M.U. cars, one of a batch of steel MP54s built in 1912. David H. Cope photo

considered the adoption of the newly developed single-phase A.C. system, it finally adopted a 650-volt D.C. third-rail system essentially identical to that employed on the Long Island, with an overhead trolley wire and trolley pole system at two locations. Car builders American Car & Foundry, J. G. Brill, and Wason built a fleet of 68 wooden M.U. cars for the new service. New passenger terminals at Camden and Atlantic City

and upgraded track were also part of the improvements.

Opened on September 18, 1906, the new electrification produced some gratifying growth in the line's passenger traffic. By the end of the first years of electric operation, business was up by 20 percent on the Camden-Atlantic City route, and by even more on the Millville branch, while commuter zone traffic in the Camden area increased by an extraordinary 250

percent. Much of the line's Atlantic City traffic was lost to automobiles in the years after World War I, and the electrification was cut back to Newfield, N.J., in 1931. Declining traffic on the remainder of the system after World War II, and a New Jersey law that brought to an end the operation of the line's obsolete wooden passenger equipment, brought an end to the remaining electric operation in 1949.

Beneath the Hudson to Manhattan

Even as its Long Island and West Jersey & Seashore subsidiaries began work on their third-rail D.C. electrifications, the Pennsylvania had already initiated what would be perhaps the single greatest improvement in the company's history. This was the extraordinary New York tunnel and terminal project that would take both the Pennsylvania and the Long Island railroads under the Hudson and East rivers to a magnificent new Manhattan terminal, and it would include what would be one of the most ambitious electrification projects yet undertaken by any American railroad.

Ever since the Pennsylvania had reached the west bank of the Hudson opposite Manhattan in 1871, the railroad had sought a way to carry its passengers right into Manhattan. As long as its New York terminal facilities were located at Jersey City, the Pennsylvania had been at a severe competitive disadvantage to its principal rival for New York passenger traffic, Commodore Vanderbilt's New York Central & Hudson River. While the Pennsylvania's passengers were obliged to transfer to ferries at Jersey City to complete a journey to New York, the Central's passengers were carried right into the railroad's splendid Grand Central Depot in the heart of Manhattan.

For close to 30 years the Pennsylvania had considered a variety of bridge and tunnel projects that might give its trains direct access to Manhattan. This would not be easy, for the Hudson River was close to a mile wide and 65 feet deep, and neither a bridge nor a tunnel crossing of that magnitude had yet been achieved by nineteenth century engineers.

As early as 1874 the Hudson Tunnel Railroad Company had begun work on an ambitious tunnel project that was to carry passenger and freight trains under the river, drawn by specially designed engines, "consuming their own steam and smoke," or powered by compressed air. Ahead of its time

both in terms of the required tunneling technology and the availability of suitable motive power, the tunnel project continued sporadically for more than 30 years before it was finally completed and opened as part of the Hudson & Manhattan rapid transit line.

The Pennsylvania had been far more interested in proposals for a Hudson River bridge. As early as 1884 bridge engineer Gustav Lindenthal had proposed an enormous suspension bridge. Over the next decade Lindenthal's plans

went through several revisions, while a rival bridge company advanced plans of its own. Shipping interests were opposed to bridge piers in the river, and the controversy eventually went all the way to the Congress, the War Department, and President Cleveland. Not until 1894 were the design conditions for a bridge finally resolved.

In 1892 the Pennsylvania's Samuel Rea, then an assistant to President George B. Roberts, had completed a study of the alterna-

tives for a Hudson crossing, recommending the choice of Lindenthal's plan for a high-level bridge. The project would cost about $100 million, and an important component of the plan recommended by Rea was the inclusion of the other New Jersey railroads in the project to help pay for it. The other railroads declined to participate, however, and the Pennsylvania was unable to proceed on its own.

The project languished until shortly after the turn of the century, when the rapidly developing

▲ Eastbound for Penn Station, New York, a DD1 swept around the long curve approaching the Bergen Hill tunnel portal with a seven-car train made up entirely of steel cars. The fresh grading of the high line embankment testified to the newness of the Pennsylvania's entry into Manhattan. David P. Morgan Library photo

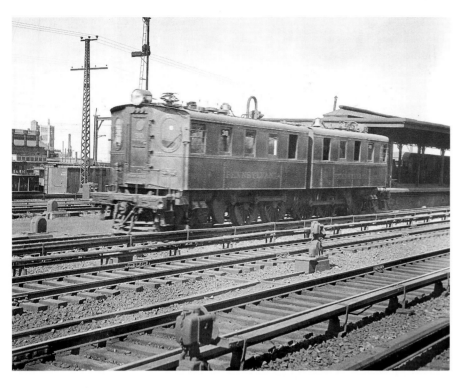

technology of electrification offered a new solution. Developed under the visionary leadership of Pennsylvania President Alexander J. Cassatt, who had taken office in 1899, this new scheme involved the construction of a new line from a point near Newark, N.J., that would pass through Bergen Hill and under the Hudson in twin tunnels to a new midtown Manhattan station. Tunnels continuing across Manhattan and under the East River to Long Island City would link the new station with the Long Island Rail Road, a new

passenger train storage and servicing yard at Sunnyside in Queens, and a future link with the New Haven Railroad by way of a planned bridge across the East River at Hell Gate. Freight traffic would move between the Pennsylvania and the New Haven by means of a new car float operation between Greenville, N.J., and Bay Ridge, in Brooklyn. A new line to be built jointly by the two roads would provide a link with the Hell Gate Bridge. Operation of the planned tunnels with steam power was not feasible. Electrification was what made the whole scheme work.

Planning for the great tunnel and terminal project began in 1901, and the first major contract for the tunneling work was awarded in June 1903. Both the Hudson and East River tunnels were complete by 1909, ready for the installation of track and electrification. Excavation of the 7.5-acre site for the splendid new Pennsylvania Station began in 1904, and the structure was substantially complete by August of 1910.

Even as the tunnel and terminal work proceeded, the Pennsylvania was carefully considering the electrification technology that would

be most suitable for the installation. In addition to the electrification projects of the Pennsylvania's LIRR and WJ&S subsidiaries, two other major electrifications were initiated in the New York area early in the new century. The New York Central & Hudson River had adopted a third-rail D.C. technology for its extensive terminal and suburban electrification, which was similar to that of the two PRR subsidiaries, but the New Haven had taken a different path for an electrification of its lines from New York to New Haven.

The New Haven had adopted the newer 11,000-volt, 25-hertz, single-phase A.C. system developed by the Westinghouse Electric & Manufacturing Company. A high-voltage alternating current installation offered the important advantage of much lower line losses than those of a low-voltage D.C. system, an important consideration for a long-distance electrification like that of the New Haven.

Pennsylvania President Cassatt had appointed an electrification committee, headed by electrical engineer George Gibbs, to develop the characteristics of its electrical installation and equipment. This committee took up the basic

◀ The days of the DD1s at the head end of the Pennsylvania's mainline limiteds were drawing to a close when two-unit DD1 EZN 37 accelerated out of Manhattan Transfer with an eastbound train for Penn Station in August 1934. The railroad's new A.C. catenary was complete, and new A.C. electrics had already been hauling some trains for a year and a half. John P. Ahrens photo

question of electrification technology in 1908. While there was already substantial experience with the low-voltage, third-rail D.C. technology, the New Haven's A.C. installation had been in operation only since mid-1907. To learn more about A.C. systems, the Pennsylvania built a test installation on 5 miles of LIRR track on a branch east of Garden City. Track was upgraded for high-speed operation, and nine types of overhead construction, as well as a dummy tunnel section, were installed for the tests. Test equipment included

an A.C. test locomotive, an A.C. motor car supplied by Westinghouse, and two work cars fitted with test pantographs.

Tests began in October 1908 with results that, according to Gibbs, "demonstrated the need of considerable further experimental work to adapt the system to the tunnel and yard conditions." For this reason, as well as to avoid complications in interchange with the third-rail electrifications of the Long Island or the new Hudson & Manhattan, the Pennsylvania decided to adopt a third-rail D.C.

system for its New York terminal electrification. Recognizing that an A.C. electrification might be an appropriate choice at a later date, however, the railroad wisely allowed for future installation of an overhead catenary system in the design for its Hudson River and East River tunnels.

Electrification work had begun long before the railroad had made its decision on an electrification technology. The first element of work was an enormous power generating station at Long Island City with a generating capacity of more than 38,000 kilowatts. Because it would also supply the Long Island electrification, construction of the plant began in 1903; it was ready to run in time for the opening of the LIRR electrification in July 1905. Work on the Pennsylvania's third-rail installation began in 1909. In addition to the Hudson and East River tunnels, the installation included the extensive new Sunnyside passenger train yard and servicing facility across the East River from Manhattan. This massive yard extended some 6½ miles west of the New Jersey tunnel portal to Manhattan Transfer, where the exchange between steam and electric motive power would be made and passengers bound to or from Jersey City or lower Manhattan could transfer between PRR and Hudson & Manhattan trains.

Initial motive power for the new electrification comprised a fleet of 24 big DD1 boxcab electric locomotives (see "The Remarkable DD1," page 24). Two DD1 prototypes delivered in 1909 and early 1910 were tested extensively before the remaining production units were completed later in 1910. Another nine DD1s were added to the fleet in 1911. The DD1s proved to be highly capable

performers that easily met the demanding conditions imposed by the steep 1.9 percent tunnel ruling grade and the high-density operations of the Pennsylvania's New York terminal.

The new tunnels, the great Pennsylvania Station in Manhattan, the Sunnyside yard facilities, tracks, signaling, and electrification were all in readiness late in 1910. The station itself was dedicated in elaborate ceremonies on August 1, 1910. Long Island Rail Road operations from the new terminal began on September 8, while Pennsylvania Railroad service into Manhattan began in November with a new timetable that called for 55 eastbound and 61 westbound trains to and from Penn Station daily. The start of service on November 27 was preceded by a two-week dress rehearsal, in which every train was run, steam and electric locomotives were exchanged at Manhattan Transfer, and trains were inspected and serviced. PRR President James McRea and other officials were on board the first train to arrive at 12:50 a.m. Opening day traffic was so heavy that the railroad operated 51 extra trains to handle the crowds. In addition to passengers, a crowd of sightseers

estimated at 100,000 wandered through the station. "In thousands they flooded the acres of its floor space, gazed like awestruck pygmies at the vaulted ceilings far above them . . . ," reported one newspaper.

At last, 39 years after it had reached the west shore of the Hudson, the Pennsylvania Railroad had attained a fully competitive position with the rival New York Central with a splendid Manhattan terminal of its own.

The Pennsylvania's later decision to adopt single-phase A.C. electrification for mainline electrification brought changes to the New York terminal installation. The first of these was the appearance of the L5 electric locomotives, an elongated steeple-cab unit with a 1-D-1 wheel arrangement that was intended to be a "universal" electric locomotive capable of both A.C. and D.C. operation. A single A.C. prototype was never repeated, but a total of 23 D.C.-equipped L5s entered Penn Station service during 1924-28. Some of the DD1s were transferred to the Long Island, while others remained in Penn Station service through the 1950s, with one durable pair continuing to operate until 1962.

▲ Restyled with new lettering and pinstriping reminiscent of the Pennsylvania's new GG1 electrics, DD1 EZN 16 was all dressed up for special service forwarding through trains from Penn Station to the 1939-40 World's Fair site in Flushing. W. R. Osborne photo

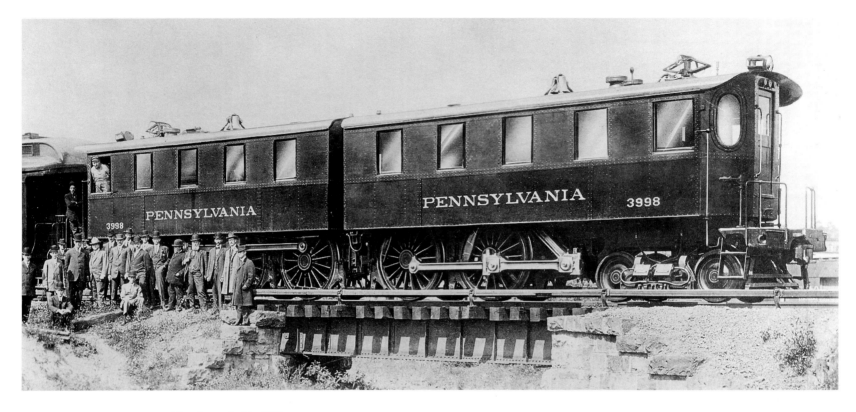

The Remarkable DD1

The electric locomotives that operated the Pennsylvania's New York tunnel and terminal electrification were developed through an extended program of study and testing. The electrification committee appointed by President Cassatt first developed two experimental 1350-h.p. locomotives that were built at the railroad's Juniata shops in Altoona, Pa., with electrical equipment supplied by Westinghouse. Both were boxcab units with a pair of motor trucks linked in an articulated B+B arrangement. One was fitted with four nose-suspended traction motors, while the other had motors of the gearless quill type. The two units were placed in test operation on the already completed LIRR electrification, where they worked well enough in low-speed operation, but developed a rhythmic side swaying at high speeds that was highly destructive to track.

Further tests were called for, and in 1907 an extensive test program was carried out on a section of the West Jersey & Seashore near Franklinville, N.J. A section of track was specially outfitted with measuring devices that could record the lateral pressure on the rails from test locomotives. In addition to the two experimental electric units, the test fleet included a 70-ton locomotive in a 2-B wheel arrangement, with a four-wheel guiding truck and

four 72-inch driving wheels, provided by Westinghouse and a Class EP-1 A.C./D.C. B-B locomotive borrowed from the New Haven's new electrification. For comparative purposes, Class D16b 4-4-0 and Class E2 4-4-2 steam locomotives were also tested.

The extensive tests revealed that the Westinghouse electric unit with the 2-B wheel arrangement was by far the best performer among the electric units, equaling the tracking qualities and stability of the steam locomotives. This was attributed to its asymmetrical wheel arrangement and high center of gravity, both characteristics that were adopted in the design of the Pennsylvania's new units for the New York tunnel and terminal electrification.

Employing the same 2-B wheel arrangement as the test unit, the new DD1 boxcab electrics were made up of two permanently coupled units, forming a 65-foot, 156.5-ton locomotive. The back-to-back 4-4-0 wheel arrangement led to the DD1 class designation, reflecting the railroad's D class 4-4-0 steam locomotives. Each unit had a single 2000-h.p. Westinghouse traction motor that was carried on a main frame above the wheels, giving the locomotive the desired high center of gravity. Cranks at each end of the motor shaft were connected by rods to a cranked jackshaft, from which side-rod connections were made to the driving wheels, as on steam locomotives.

Built in the Pennsylvania's Juniata Shops at Altoona, and provided with electrical equipment supplied by Westinghouse, the DD1s proved to be prodigious performers. In dynamometer tests a two-unit DD1 proved capable of a starting tractive effort of 79,200 pounds, and their maximum safe speed was 80 m.p.h. While specifications for the locomotives required that they be able to start and accelerate a 550-ton train on the ruling 1.93 percent tunnel grade, they proved capable of handling an 850-ton train under these conditions. The DD1 was truly, as writer Frederick Westing so aptly termed it in the October 1956 *Trains,* "the locomotive that made Penn Station possible."

▲ (left) This is what a DD1 looked like with the boxcab removed. Each of the big 650-volt D.C. Westinghouse motors generated 2000 h.p. Mounting the motors above the frame gave the DD1s the high center of gravity that the Pennsylvania's tests had shown would contribute to good tracking and riding qualities. David P. Morgan Library photo

▲ Elongated, rounded end windows and a roof overhang gave the DD1 a distinctive appearance. Each two-unit DD1 was assigned its own Electric Zone Number. EZN 26 was made up of units 3984 and 3985. David P. Morgan Library photo

Pennsylvania Station

The capstone to the Pennsylvania's New York tunnel and terminal project was the magnificent Pennsylvania Station. It would rank as one of the world's greatest railroad terminals, and electrification made it possible. The station was erected on a two-city-block site extending between Seventh and Eighth Avenues and 31st and 33rd Streets in midtown Manhattan. More than 100 houses were cleared from the 8-acre site, and nearly a half million cubic yards of earth were excavated for the building and its below-ground facilities. The subterranean track level of the station covered 28 acres and included some 16 miles of track. Eleven platforms served 21 tracks.

The station's architect, Charles Follen McKim of New York's McKim, Mead & White partnership, turned to Roman models for design guidance. The exterior was executed in the Doric order and built with pink Milford granite from Massachusetts. The Seventh Avenue façade was a colonnade inspired by Giovanni Bernini's Tuscan colonnade surrounding the piazza of St. Peter's at Rome. The great vaulted main waiting room, patterned after the *tepidarium* of the Baths of Caracalla, was the largest railroad station waiting room in the world, with a floor area of more than 30,000 square feet and a ceiling 150 feet high.

◄ A closer view of the Seventh Avenue façade shows the entablature by sculptor Adolph A. Weinman that surmounted the main entrance to Penn Station. A wreath of marble surrounding the 6-foot-diameter clock was flanked by the figures of two maidens representing day and night, and six American eagles. Pennsylvania State Archives (MG-286, Penn Central Railroad Collection)

The concourse was roofed with an intricate supporting structure of open-latticed steel arches forming a glass roof of intersecting arches suggestive of the trainsheds of European stations. One writer described the station as "the outward and visible sign of a triumph hidden under the waters of the Hudson River."

The station's design was likened to a "monumental bridge" over the tracks, 40 to 50 feet below street level, with the station's facilities stacked in layers above the tracks.

Passengers descended from entrances at street level to a lower waiting room and concourse level and then descended again to reach the platforms.

By 1919 Penn Station accommodated almost 35 million passengers annually. By 1939 this had doubled to almost 70 million. The traffic of World War II provided the ultimate test of the Pennsylvania's great station and its carefully planned circulation system and vast public rooms. In 1945, the busiest wartime year, more than

109 million travelers passed through the station. An average of 350,000 passengers passed through the station every day, and more than 900 trains arrived and departed.

Penn Station fell on hard times in the years after the war, as the railroad passenger business began its long decline. With its Penn Station operating and upkeep expenses far outstripping the available revenues, the Pennsylvania began looking for a way out. Plans to tear the station down and

▶ Modeled after the *tepidarium* of the Baths of Caracalla, Penn Station's main waiting room was the world's largest, with a floor area of more than 30,000 square feet, and its great vaulted ceiling was 150 feet high. Courtesy of Hagley Museum and Library (Neg. 72.432.2)

▶▶ The Penn Station concourse was roofed with this intricate supporting structure of open latticed steel arches forming a glass roof of intersecting barrel arches said to be reminiscent of the trainsheds of European stations. The walls were finished in granite. Eighteen train gates and stairs led to the platform level, 28 feet below. This view dates to 1961. Don Wood photo

replace it with profitable real estate development led to one of the first great battles of the historic preservation movement. The battle was lost, and in 1963 the station began to come down, to be replaced by a new Madison Square Garden and an office building. Station facilities were relegated to a below-ground concourse that seemed little better than a large subway station.

By the beginning of the new century, however, Penn Station was on the way back to something like its one-time grandeur. A revitalized Amtrak Northeast Corridor and surging commuter traffic from the New Jersey and Long Island suburbs had brought traffic through the station to levels that hadn't been seen for a half century. Both the Long Island Rail Road and New Jersey Transit had under-

taken major improvement and expansion of their facilities in the station, while work was underway on a conversion of the classical James A. Farley post office building on Eighth Avenue, itself designed by McKim, Mead & White, into a grand new Amtrak intercity terminal reminiscent of the original Penn Station.

◀ Until it was later closed in, one could look down through the main concourse all the way to track level, some 40 to 50 feet below street level. David P. Morgan Library photo

▲ World War II brought record traffic levels to Penn Station. In its busiest wartime year—1945—the station saw an average of 350,000 arriving or departing passengers and more than 900 trains every day. Associated Press photo

Under A.C. Catenary

▶ Pennsylvania Railroad A.C. electric operation began in 1915 with electrification of its Main Line suburban service between Broad Street Station in Philadelphia and suburban Paoli. These early Paoli line MP54 multiple-unit cars seen eastbound at Wynnewood, Pa., were rebuilt for electric service from steel P54 coaches originally built for steam-powered suburban services. Pennsylvania Railroad photo

Even before the great New York tunnel and terminal electrification was complete, the Pennsylvania had turned its attention to still other prospective electrification.

First to come under consideration was the railroad's main line between Philadelphia and Pittsburgh, which had seen a phenomenal growth in both passenger and freight traffic. Completion of the Trenton Cutoff around Philadelphia in 1892 and construction of the Low Grade Line between the Philadelphia area and Harrisburgh early in the century had relieved the growing congestion at the east end of the main

line, but the railroad's arduous crossing of the Alleghenies was approaching capacity. The four-track main route over the mountains at Altoona, which included the famous Horseshoe Curve, had already been supplemented by double-tracking of the New Portage Branch, which provided an alternate route to Horseshoe Curve on the east slope of the mountains. Construction of still another line was considered, but was found to be prohibitively expensive.

Extensive studies of electrification of both the Low Grade Line and the route over the Alleghenies were initiated as early as 1908. While both electrifications looked

promising, the railroad was not yet ready to proceed with quite so ambitious a project. By 1913 a much more modest electrification of a shorter segment over the summit was under consideration, but this, too, failed to materialize.

By this time the Pennsylvania's electrification interest had shifted to its heavily used suburban services out of Philadelphia. As early as 1912 the railroad was considering electric operation of these services to alleviate growing congestion in its Broad Street station and on the main lines. A start to the work was authorized a year later, and the first electrified suburban route began operating between Broad Street and suburban Paoli,

on the Main Line west of Philadelphia, in 1915. The Chestnut Hill branch came next, early in 1918. Other Philadelphia-area suburban electrification followed through 1930, most importantly on the New York-Philadelphia-Washington main line northward to Trenton, N.J., and southward to Wilmington, Del. The same low-voltage D.C. third-rail system employed at New York and on the West Jersey & Seashore would have been suitable for these projects as well. But by 1913 the Pennsylvania was seriously considering

its several possible mainline electrifications, and the system adopted for suburban service would have to be suitable for this as well. The superior characteristics of single-phase A.C. for long-distance electrification had by this time been convincingly demonstrated on the New Haven's New York-New Haven electrification, and the Pennsylvania wisely adopted the same system for its Philadelphia installations. These electrified commuter services were operated with a new fleet of standard MP54 multiple-unit cars (see "The Ubiq-

uitous MP54," page 90) that would eventually number more than 500.

As its Philadelphia suburban electrification expanded, the Pennsylvania continued to consider an eventual mainline electrification. By the mid-1920s the PRR's interest in mainline electrification had shifted from its route across the Pennsylvania mountains to the eastern main lines between New York and Washington, which by this time were carrying the heaviest combined passenger and freight traffic on the entire railroad. Despite the availability of a

◀ The O1s proved to be too light for many of the Pennsylvania's trains, which may explain why this eight-car suburban train near Philadelphia was double-headed by two of the 2-B-2 electrics. C. A. Brown photo

multiple-track main line, with four tracks all the way from New York to Wilmington, the Pennsylvania anticipated that continuing traffic growth would require the development of still greater capacity through either the construction of additional tracks or electrification.

Studies of the potential cost and benefits of electrification for these eastern lines promised substantial benefits, and by 1928 the Pennsylvania was ready to proceed. Following approval by the board of directors, President William Wallace Atterbury on October 23, 1928, announced what would be the largest single electrification program yet undertaken anywhere in the world. The Pennsylvania would electrify the eastern main line from New York to Wilmington, as well as the Low Grade Line west of Philadelphia to Columbia, Pa., comprising a total of some 325 route-miles and 1300 track-miles, and it would acquire a new fleet of 365 new electric freight and passenger locomotives. More than 500 daily passenger trains would be operated with electric power. The project would cost an estimated $100 million, and it would be completed over a period of six to seven years. "No construction of such proportions has been attempted by an American railroad in a long while," commented *The New York Times.*

Only a year later even this ambitious program was expanded with a decision to extend the electrification all the way to Washington, with an electrified connection to Potomac Yard in Alexandria, Va., for freight traffic. The cost of this enlarged program was placed at $175 million. Some 60 freight and

▲ Photographs of the Pennsylvania's boxcab P5a locomotives in passenger service are relatively rare. Although originally designed for heavy passenger trains, they proved to have serious shortcomings in high-speed operation, and were displaced to freight service as the newer GG1s were delivered. This undated view from the early 1930s shows one of the boxcab units at speed with a long train of P70 coaches on the New York Division, probably between Rahway and Elizabeth, N.J. Herbert H. Harwood Jr. Collection.

830 passenger trains, it was estimated, would operate over this great electrification each day.

Typical of the railroad that called itself "the standard railroad of the world," the Pennsylvania adopted the highest technical standards for the work. The overhead distribution system developed for the PRR lines employed a compound catenary system supported by a cross-catenary support system carried on steel H-section poles, which also carried power transmission and signal power lines. Power purchased from utility companies was delivered to

the system at four locations, where frequency converters converted the power supply from the utilities' standard 60-hertz to the 25-hertz frequency required for the PRR installation. Transformer stations stepped this power supply up to 132,000 volts for transmission to substations at intervals of 7 to 10 miles along the line, where it was stepped down to the trolley wire voltage of 11,000 volts.

The L5 electric locomotive developed several years earlier was deemed unsuitable for the demands of long-distance electric operation, and the Pennsylvania began an extensive development and test program that would produce a new fleet of single-phase A.C. electric locomotives of unprecedented capacity (see "The Pennsylvania's Electric Locomotives," page 92).

Still other major improvements were made to the eastern main lines concurrently with the electrification. The entire signal system was reconstructed and converted to position light signals for the higher speeds that would become possible with electrification. Telephone and telegraph lines were rearranged and placed in below-ground conduits to eliminate electrical interference from the overhead catenary. A number of

bridges over the tracks were raised by anywhere from 6 inches to 3 feet to provide adequate catenary clearance. Both a new through station at 30th Street and a new Suburban Station were built at Philadelphia, while a new station was constructed at Newark, N.J. Many grade crossings were eliminated, and new tunnels were built at Baltimore. Many miles of track were reballasted and relaid with the Pennsylvania's new 152-pound rail section in preparation for the higher speeds that electrification would bring.

Scarcely had the Pennsylvania begun work on its costly electrification than the nation was plunged into a great national depression following the stock market crash of October 1929. Instead of curtailing the work, however, the railroad pressed ahead. Early in 1931, President Atterbury even announced that the work would be accelerated, completing in 2½ years work that the railroad had originally planned to do in four. The railroad was able to finance the work itself through 1931 but then sought the aid of newly established federal programs. A $27.5 million loan from the Reconstruction Finance Corporation in 1932 and an $80 million loan from the Public Works Administration in 1934 helped to keep the work moving ahead at a fast pace.

By the time electrification reached its peak in mid-1934, the Pennsylvania had 76 work trains and 12,000 men employed on the project, and it was estimated that at least as many more men were engaged in the manufacture of equipment and supplies.

Electric operation began in stages as the project was completed. The first section to be converted was the original New York tunnel and terminal D.C. third-rail electrification extending from Sunnyside Yard through Penn Station to Manhattan Transfer, which was shifted to A.C. operation early in 1932, while multiple-unit local train service began operating as far south as New Brunswick, N.J., later in the year.

Work was complete all the way to Philadelphia early in 1933, and the departure of the first train to operate between New York and Philadelphia under electric power was marked by a festive event at Penn Station on the morning of January 16. New York City Mayor John P. O'Brien and Pennsylvania vice president George LeBoutillier attended. As the 9 a.m. departure

time approached, a bugler from the Sixteenth U.S. Infantry blew the command "stand by," followed by "forward." Mayor O'Brien then cut a ceremonial ribbon and the bugler blew "double time" as the train began to move.

"A crowd of Long Island commuters watched the proceedings from another platform," reported *The New York Times*. "While uncertain of its significance, they gave a cheer as the Philadelphia-bound train pulled out."

Through electric operation between New York and Wilmington began a month later, but it was almost two years more before the final segment between Wilmington and Washington was ready. With this last section virtually complete, the Pennsylvania celebrated with a special run from Washington to Philadelphia and return behind prototype GG1 electric locomotive 4800 on January 28, 1935. On board the nine-car train were Secretary of the Interior Harold Ickes, PRR vice president Martin W. Clement, and nearly 130 public officials, railroad men, and newsmen. Running time for the entire 269-mile round trip was just 212 minutes, for an average speed of better than 75 m.p.h. On the return trip, the GG1

and its train reached a maximum speed of 102 m.p.h. and recorded the fastest trip made until that time between Philadelphia and Washington, with a running time of just 1 hour 50 minutes.

Regular electric operation between New York and Washington began less than two weeks later, on February 10, with the 4 p.m. departure of GG1 4800 from Washington's Union Station with the northbound *Congressional Limited* for New York. A crowd estimated at a thousand crowded the Union Station platforms, while hundreds more

▲ As indicated by this 1935 view of a New York-Washington train, one of the chief shortcomings of the P5a was insufficient power to make the 3-hour-35-minute running time between the two cities with a long, heavy train without double-heading. The larger, more powerful GG1s could handle these schedules with ease, and the P5a units were soon relegated to freight service. Bert Pennypacker photo

▲ The modified P5a units with a streamlined center-cab configuration lasted in passenger service a little longer than their boxcab sisters. Altoona-built 4788 headed the New York-bound *Legislator* near Zoo Tower in Philadelphia in March 1935. David P. Morgan Library photo

watched the departure of the 14-car train from the New York Avenue bridge. So many had booked space on the southbound *Congressional*, which departed from New York's Penn Station a half hour later, that the train operated in two sections. All passenger trains between the two cities were operating under electric power by March 15. The shift of freight operations to electric operation began in May 1935 and was complete by June.

The results of electric operation proved even greater than the Pennsylvania had anticipated.

Operating expenses were substantially lower than they had been with steam power. Running times between New York and Washington were substantially reduced; by April 1936, for example, the schedule of the crack *Congressional* had been cut from 4 hours 15 minutes with steam power to only 3 hours 35 minutes. By the end of 1936 New York-Washington passenger revenues were up by almost 6 percent. The faster electric freight service enabled the Pennsylvania to offer third-morning rather than fourth-morning delivery of Florida perishables to New York. Electrification so increased the capacity of the line that earlier plans to expand the main line to six tracks through Elizabeth, N.J., and to build a new line and bridge at Trenton were found to be unnecessary.

By January 1937 the Pennsylvania was ready to take another giant step in electrification, and its board of directors approved a $50 million plan to extend catenary west to Harrisburg over the main line used by passenger trains and to complete electrification of the Low Grade Line used by most freight traffic all the way to Enola Yard. Also included were the largely freight lines between

Monmouth Junction and South Amboy, N.J., and the Susquehanna River line between Perryville, Md., on the New York-Washington line, and a junction with the Low Grade Line at Columbia. The work went swiftly, and the main line to Harrisburg was ready for the opening of electric passenger operation on January 15, 1938. The westbound *Metropolitan*, running behind GG1 4863, made the inaugural run with electric power.

"Whistles shrieked, crowds cheered, and the Metropolitan Express, first electric train traveling between Philadelphia and Harrisburg, glided out of Broad Street Station on Saturday morning to mark another epoch in the history of rail transportation in this locality," reported the Harrisburg *Patriot*.

"Sirens Go to Town as P.R.R. Electric Goes to Harrisburg," headlined the *Philadelphia Inquirer*. "It sounded like all the whistles in the world—like New Year's Eve, the first Armistice Day and the crack of doom all rolled into one package," continued the *Inquirer*'s enthusiastic reporter. "Every locomotive in the city, whether it was pulling passenger cars, freight, or just idling in the yards, joined in the screeching

farewell to Engineer W.O. Buck and his 13-car train."

All along the route thousands lined the tracks at station platforms and crossings to watch the *Metropolitan*'s passage, and thousands more greeted the train's arrival at Harrisburg, eight minutes ahead of schedule. Within weeks all of the railroad's east-west through passenger trains were moving under electric power east of Harrisburg, while the conversion of freight traffic to electric power was completed on April 15.

The Pennsylvania Railroad now had some 673 route-miles and 2158 track-miles operating under electric power. This represented fully a third of all U.S. electrification and nearly 10 percent of the world total. The Pennsylvania Railroad had completed the greatest railroad electrification in the world.

A study of the benefits of the electrification showed annual savings for 1938 in motive power operating costs of more than $7.7 million. The running times of east-west through trains were significantly reduced. Electrification enabled the Pennsylvania to reduce the running time of its premier New York-Chicago *Broadway* *Limited* from 17 hours to only 16 hours in June 1938, and within another two years five other trains were operating on New York-Chicago timings of only 17 hours. Freight running times between Enola Yard at Harrisburg and the New York terminals were reduced an average of 2 hours.

Over the next few years the benefits of electrification were to show themselves in different and even more important ways as the U.S. entered World War II. The industrialized eastern states produced an enormous volume of war materiel, and the eastern seaboard became

the main staging area for the war against the Axis powers of Europe. Between 1939 and 1944 the Pennsylvania's overall freight traffic more than doubled and its passenger traffic quadrupled. Electric operation provided the enormous increase in capacity that was needed to move this unprecedented flood of wartime traffic over the railroad's vital eastern main lines.

In the decade after the war, the Pennsylvania began the development of new generations of electric locomotives and multiple-unit rolling stock. A 1949 test with a standard MP54 M.U. car equipped with ignitron-rectifiers and D.C. traction motors paved the way for a new fleet of rectifier locomotives (see "The Pennsylvania's Electric Locomotives," page 92), and a new generation of modern M.U. cars.

Six prototype Class MP85 M.U.s built by the Budd Company in 1958 employed the builder's lightweight *Pioneer III* stainless-steel car body and were fitted with two ignitron-rectifier tubes and four D.C. traction motors that provided a maximum speed of 90 m.p.h. Dozens of similar Silverliner cars were added to the Pennsylvania roster in subsequent years, gradually pushing the venerable MP54 fleet into retirement.

◀ Demonstrating the extraordinary power and speed of the GG1, prototype 4800 raced through Loudon Park, Md., with the 17-car *Colonial* from Boston and New York on May 31, 1937. Charles B. Chaney, Smithsonian Institution (Neg. 22154).

So impressed were the Pennsylvania's motive power officials with the performance of the new Silverliners that they turned to the ignitron-rectifier M.U. car as the basis for a new high-speed train program that was intended eventually to replace the GG1 fleet in Northeast Corridor service. A series of 100-m.p.h. tests on the New York-Washington line soon after the prototype M.U. cars were delivered produced some promising results. Passage of the federal High Speed Ground Transportation Research and Development Act in 1965 led to the development of a $55 million joint PRR-U.S. Government project with a goal of 150-m.p.h. operation in the New York-Washington corridor. More high-speed tests with four special test cars on upgraded track between Trenton and New Brunswick followed in 1966-67, but even before then the Pennsylvania had placed an order with Budd for 50 high-speed Metroliner M.U. cars that were to be capable of a maximum speed of 160 m.p.h.

Largely because of the haste with which they were rushed into production, without benefit of either the test program results or careful prototype testing, start-up

▲ The splendid new electrics had only been in service for a few months when GG1 4813 was recorded at speed with a heavy northbound train 10 miles out of Washington Union Station in the fall of 1935. No. 4813 was one of 14 GG1s completed between May and August 1935 at General Electric's Erie, Pa., works. General Electric photo

of the Pennsylvania's new high-speed Metroliner service was delayed again and again as the railroad struggled to overcome electrical and mechanical problems with the new equipment. Long before the trains were ready the curtain rang down on the great Pennsylvania Railroad. Faced with declining freight traffic and burdened by an excess of unprofitable passenger services, the Pennsylva-

nia early in 1968 entered into an ill-starred merger with the New York Central, and to the new Penn Central Company and—as it turned out—to *its* Amtrak successor would fall the continuing development of North America's greatest electrification.

◀ In an early view of GG1 operation, No. 4815 accelerates out of
30th Street Station in Philadelphia
with a heavy southbound limited in
July 1936. No. 4815 was assem-
bled at the Pennsylvania's Altoona
shops with mechanical components
from Baldwin and electrical equipment from Westinghouse. General
Electric photo

▲ The distinctive streamlined
styling of the GG1 is evident in this
photograph at Penn Station,
Newark. Pennsylvania Railroad,
A. F. Sozio photo

▶ As the Pennsylvania's growing GG1 fleet took over mainline passenger operations, the P5a's, regeared for lower-speed freight service, assumed duties as the railroad's principal electric freight motive power. One of them headed a southbound freig ht passing Brill Tower in Philadelphia in September 1935. General Electric photo

▶▶ The Pennsylvania's fleet of streamlined, center-cab modified P5a's also ended up in the freight pool. Two of them headed a northbound freight through Halethorpe, Md., on the four-track main line. Frank Clodfelter photo

▶ Geared down for greater pulling power instead of speed, the GG1 could acquit itself as a powerful freight hauler as well as a high-speed passenger locomotive. Somewhere on the four-track New York-Washington main line one of the big electrics powered a fast freight soon after their introduction. General Electric photo

▶▶ Southbound for Washington with a heavy train of Pullmans, GG1 4850 emerged from beneath New York's General Post Office on the way from Penn Station to the Hudson River tubes. No. 4850 was one of 18 GG1s completed by the Pennsylvania's Altoona shops in 1935. Frank Clodfelter photo

▶ The long run through the Hudson River tubes and under Bergen Hill complete, GG1 4926 emerged from the Bergen Hill tunnel portal with a westbound Lehigh Valley train. The electric would hand the train over to Lehigh Valley power at Hunter Tower, just beyond Newark. Bruce Owen Nett photo

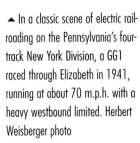

▲ In a classic scene of electric rail-
roading on the Pennsylvania's four-
track New York Division, a GG1
raced through Elizabeth in 1941,
running at about 70 m.p.h. with a
heavy westbound limited. Herbert
Weisberger photo

▲ Eastbound towards New York,
P5a 4757 rolled through Elizabeth
in April 1941 with a long freight
train. Herbert Weisberger photo

◀ Pennsylvania Railroad electrification reached its full scope on January 15, 1938, when trains began operating under catenary between Philadelphia and Harrisburg, Pa. This was the scene at the Harrisburg station as a large crowd awaited the departure of GG1s 4862 and 4863 with the first scheduled eastbound train and the special train that had brought Pennsylvania officials and members of the press from Philadelphia. Al Rung photo

◀◀ Between Wilmington and Baltimore, the Pennsylvania main line crossed the Susquehanna River at Havre de Grace, Md., on this 3269-foot, double-track deck truss bridge. GG1 4821 hurried across the span with a northbound 14-car train of heavy steel cars. David P. Morgan Library photo

▶ In addition to its New York-Washington mainline electrification, the Pennsylvania erected 11,000-volt A.C. catenary over a portion of the New York & Long Branch line that carried heavy traffic to the New Jersey shore. Bound from New York to Bay Head Junction on the coast, a first section of train 787 left the main line at Rahway for the New York & Long Branch on a sunny June afternoon in 1947. Heading the long train of P70 coaches was GG1 4901, which would turn the train over to steam power at South Amboy. Arthur F. Knauer photo

◀ In a winter view of Washington Union Station dating from the late 1930s, a departing GG1 with a northbound train is framed in the window of interlocking tower K. Pennsylvania Railroad photo

▲ The Pennsylvania's premier train, the all-Pullman New York-Chicago *Broadway Limited,* was reequipped with new streamlined rolling stock in 1938. GG1s powered the train at speeds up to 100 m.p.h. for the New York-Harrisburg leg of the *Broadway*'s overnight run. No. 4892 headed the train east of Metuchen, N.J., on the New York Division four-track main line. Pennsylvania Railroad photo

▶ The Trenton Cutoff, which extended from a junction with the Main Line west of Philadelphia to join the Philadelphia-New York main line at Morrisville, Pa., provided a bypass around the congested Philadelphia area for Pennsylvania freights. P5a 4706 pulled an eastbound freight onto the beginning of the Cutoff at Thorndale in November 1947. In the foreground are tracks 1 and 2 of the Main Line, while tracks 3 and 4 are on the opposite side of the Cutoff embankment. Charles A. Elston photo

▶ For decades on end the annual post-Thanksgiving Day Army-Navy football game at Philadelphia's Municipal Stadium was the occasion for a heavy traffic in special trains on the Pennsylvania. This was the lineup of GG1-powered specials waiting at South Philadelphia to begin the return trip from the game on December 1, 1951. John F. Endler Jr. photo

◄ For several generations of New York-bound New Jersey commuters the Pennsylvania's sturdy MP54s provided daily home-to-work transportation in its busy Trenton-New York local service. A five-car train of the tuscan red M.U.s passed Nassau Tower as the train accelerated away from the Princeton Junction stop in 1952. Herbert H. Harwood Jr. photo

▶ A seven-car westbound train of MP54 multiple-unit cars gathered speed as it departed from a station stop at Colonia, N.J., on October 24, 1941. The rear two cars, a motor-trailer set, bear PRR's short-lived Futura lettering. Herb Weisgerber photo.

▶▶ A pair of the Pennsylvania's prototype E3b ignitron-rectifier electrics headed a 60-car symbol freight MD-12 north through Odenton, Md., in September 1953, en route from Potomac Yard at Alexandria, Va., to Philadelphia. While an order for new electric freight power was still several years away, the performance of these Westinghouse-built prototypes helped set the stage for the Pennsylvania's future fleet of rectifier locomotives. H. N. Proctor photo

▶ In 1952 the Pennsylvania reequipped the premier trains operating over the electrified eastern main line, the New York-Washington *Congressional Limited* and the Boston-Washington *Senator*, with new Budd-built stainless-steel rolling stock. GG1 4909, refinished in tuscan red in place of the railroad's standard dark Brunswick green, headed the maiden northbound trip of the *Congressional* as it passed through Philadelphia on March 17, 1952. Rail Photo Service, Wayne P. Ellis photo

▲ Two GG1s teamed up at Baltimore's Penn Station in September 1954 to haul Chicago-Washington train 58, the *Liberty Limited*, on the last leg of its journey into Washington Union Station. Having arrived from Harrisburg over the former Northern Central, the train was then hauled rear end first from Baltimore to Washington, accounting for the presence of the observation car behind the locomotives. H. N. Proctor photo

▶ Northbound from Washington with Boston-bound train 176, the *Senator*, GG1 No. 4908 kicked up a wake of snow as it raced through Odenton on the center track in January 1954. H. N. Proctor photo

▶▶ The Pennsylvania's electrified main line across northeastern Maryland crossed the Susquehanna River and several broad estuaries from Chesapeake Bay on long bridges. This was the crossing of the Bush River estuary north of Edgewood, Md. GG1 4845 headed a long train southbound from New York to Washington in September 1954. James P. Gallagher photo

▶ Among the most impressive of Pennsylvania Railroad bridges was this crossing of the Schuylkill River at Philadelphia. Rebuilt several times, it was last reconstructed during 1911-14, when an iron center span was replaced by stone arches and the structure was widened to accommodate five tracks. Tuscan red GG1 4913 with the northbound *Morning Congressional* crossed it on the way to the North Philadelphia station and New York on December 17, 1957. David G. Knox photo

◀ The 1950s were a time of much experimentation in new passenger train designs. The Pennsylvania tried the Budd Company's radical low-center-of-gravity tubular train. GG1 4883 powered the eight-car stainless-steel train for this classic publicity photograph taken shortly before the train entered New York-Washington service as *The Keystone* in June 1956. Pennsylvania Railroad photo

◀ GG1s 4841 and 4816 headed a heavy northbound freight across the massive Susquehanna River bridge at Havre de Grace in September 1956. James P. Gallagher photo

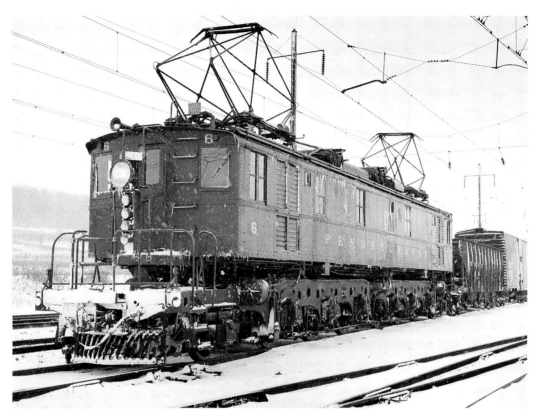

◀◀ Moments out of Philadelphia's 30th Street Station in 1958, the northbound *Mid-Day Congressional* accelerated towards Zoo Junction and the Schuylkill River crossing on its high-speed dash to New York. In the center background can be seen the sprawling Penn coach yard and 30th Street Station, while to the right is the elevated "high line," which carried Pennsylvania freights through central Philadelphia. Aaron G. Fryer photo

◀ In 1956 the Pennsylvania, in a major departure from its normal motive power acquisition policy, purchased eight used 1-C+C-1 locomotives from the Great Northern's discontinued Cascade Tunnel electrification in Washington. Designated PRR Class FF2, these big motor-generator boxcab units were placed in helper and road freight service on the main line west of Philadelphia. No. 6 headed a Lancaster, Pa.-bound freight in a heavy snowstorm at Thorndale, Pa., on February 1, 1958. Don Wood photo

◀ A single P5a — No. 4741 — entered the Trenton Cutoff at Thorndale on February 1, 1958, with eastbound symbol freight NY-8 for New York. Don Wood photo

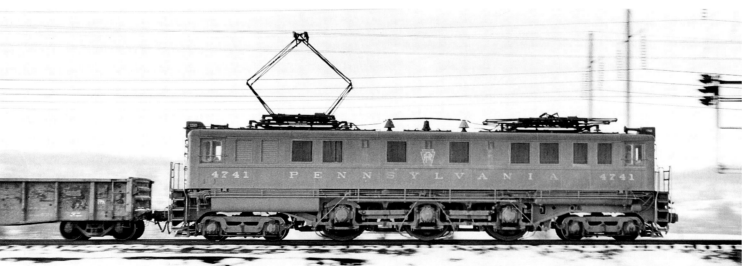

▶ A shuttle train of MP54s made the connection between Princeton Junction and nearby Princeton, N.J., for Pennsylvania commuters. Passengers from the New York area boarded the shuttle at the junction on a cold afternoon in February 1958. Jim Shaughnessy photo

▶ In late March of 1958 the Pennsylvania struggled to maintain service in the midst of a heavy, wet snowfall that hit the Philadelphia area. At Overbrook on the morning of March 20 a westbound Paoli local crossed over from an emergency routing on an eastbound track that was required because of dead wire on the normal westbound route. Aaron G. Fryer photo

▶▶ By the morning of March 21 the storm had begun to abate. Trackmen clearing switches at Overbrook stood back as one of the Pennsylvania's eastbound passenger fleet came through behind a GG1. Aaron G. Fryer photo

▸ The vanguard of a new fleet of MP85 multiple-unit cars that would eventually sidetrack the enduring MP54s showed up in 1958, when Budd delivered six of these Silverliner cars based upon the builder's new *Pioneer III* stainless-steel car body design. Running as Paoli-Philadelphia train 338, a two-car train of the new M.U.s made a station stop at Overbrook on July 29, 1958. Aaron G. Fryer photo

◄ Triple-headed P5a boxcabs, headed by No. 4734, provided a prodigious 16,800-h.p. peak output to power this eastbound freight for New York at Monmouth Junction, N.J., in April 1960. Alfred R. Jaeger photo

▼ A much-watched train was this special, which carried premier Nikita Khrushchev and a Soviet delegation from New York to Washington on September 17, 1959. GG1s 4910 and 4905 powered the 15-car train of *Congressional* equipment, seen here crossing the Kearny Meadows just outside Harrison, N.J. Don Wood photo

▶ New York's Pennsylvania Station was an intensely busy place at almost any time of day. At 2:30 p.m. on a November day in 1961 a Washington express, with through cars for southern destinations, heads out from under the station's Tower A at right, while to the left an inbound MP54 M.U. local arrives from New Brunswick. At left, a New Haven EP-5 electric lays over between runs. David Plowden photo

▶ A panned photograph captured an enduring image of GG1 speed as No. 4877 raced up the center track near Bowie, Md., with a northbound train for New York in April 1963. William D. Middleton photo

◀ The old ways sometimes lasted long, even on the most modern of railroads. As late as the date of this April 6, 1963, photograph, a crossing watchman emerged from his shanty with a stop sign every time a train passed through Seabrook, Md. The GG1 was northbound with a Florida-New York train. William D. Middleton photo

◀ A westbound Paoli local required only two MP54s to accommodate midday crowds. The train was approaching the Main Line station at suburban Radnor in April 1964. William D. Middleton photo

▶ Eastbound over the Pennsylvania's original section of A.C. catenary, GG1 4890 passed through Radnor, Pa., in April 1964 with an overnight train from the west. William D. Middleton photo

◄ The Pennsylvania's high-performance Silverliner M.U.s got a new assignment in 1965 when they were placed in an experimental high-speed service between Philadelphia and Harrisburg. Seen westbound at Atglen, Pa., this two-car preview press trip on November 29, 1965, exceeded 80-m.p.h. speeds to make the 103-mile run in 1 hour 40 minutes, with five intermediate stops. David G. Knox photo

▶ Photographer Richard Steinheimer, riding in the lead unit rear cab of double-headed GG1s, recorded this fresh perspective of the celebrated electrics' classic Raymond Loewy styling. The train was westbound symbol freight CB-1 on the main line east of Harrisburg in November 1965. Richard Steinheimer photo

◄ Led by first-of-its-class No. 4400, triple-headed E44 rectifier units headed a train over the Pennsylvania's freight-only Columbia Branch east of Harrisburg in 1965. Richard Steinheimer photo

◄◄ Triple-headed GG1s headed for the B&P tunnel just west of Penn Station, Baltimore, with a westbound freight in June 1966. Just beyond the lead unit is the North Avenue viaduct, while the tunnel portal is to the left. Herbert H. Harwood Jr. photo

▲ Heading through the heart of the city, triple-headed E44s passed the Pennsylvania's Penn Station, Baltimore (at right rear), making a run for the B&P tunnel grade at B&P Junction in March 1966. Herbert H. Harwood Jr. photo

▶ Departing from Washington Union Station with train 132, the *Representative*, for New York, GG1 4919 accelerated past interlocking tower K, just north of the station in November 1967. William D. Middleton photo

◄ This GG1 trio could have developed a peak output of as much as 24,000 h.p. to move its 142-car train. The train was symbol freight MD-18, passing through the interlocking at Landover, Md., on November 10, 1967, en route from Potomac Yard, across the Potomac in Virginia, to New Jersey points. William D. Middleton photo

▶ Double-headed GG1s thundered down the center track at Bowie, Md., on November 11, 1967, with northbound train 172, the *Senator*, for New York and Boston. Bowie Tower, at left, controlled the junction with the Pennsylvania's Popes Creek Branch. William D. Middleton photo

▶▶ Models forecast the appearance of the Pennsylvania's new high-speed, multiple-unit Metroliner trains in 1967. By the time the trains entered service the railroad had disappeared into the Penn Central merger, and PC emblems had replaced the PRR keystones on the fast trains. Lawrence S. Williams, Inc, photo

Maintenance and Service Bases for the Pennsylvania's Electric Fleet

▶ Once their runs were completed at New York's Pennsylvania Station, the trains of the Pennsylvania's electric-powered passenger fleet continued on through the East River tubes to the railroad's massive maintenance, service, and storage yard at Sunnyside in Queens. In this August 1955 view a GG1 has just emerged from the tunnels to turn its train on the loop into Sunnyside Yard. The Manhattan skyline looms beyond the Long Island Rail Road's Harold Tower at the center. James G. La Vake photo

▶▶ At the Sunnyside engine terminal a hostler was bringing a GG1 from the inspection pits to the wash rack at the left, while GG1s ready for outbound assignments were lined up to the right. James G. La Vake photo

▶ Servicing of the high-mileage GG1 fleet went on around the clock at the Sunnyside engine terminal. Half a dozen of the big electrics were being readied for service in this April 1960 scene. Jim Shaughnessy photo

◀ Two earlier generations of Pennsylvania electrics waited for duty at the Sunnyside engine terminal in September 1960. At left is a pair of the DD1 electrics that inaugurated service into Pennsylvania Station in 1910, while at right is B1 class O-C-O switcher 5694 of 1935. Jim Shaughnessy photo

◀ A relatively infrequent sight under PRR catenary was the O1 class 2-B-2 passenger electric. Only eight were built before the railroad decided it needed a larger unit. No. 7853, a Class O1c unit built at Altoona and fitted with GE electrical equipment in 1931, was in the twilight of its 30-year career when this photograph was made at the Sunnyside engine terminal on an April night in 1960. Little more than a year later, the boxcab electric had been retired and sold for scrap. Jim Shaughnessy photo

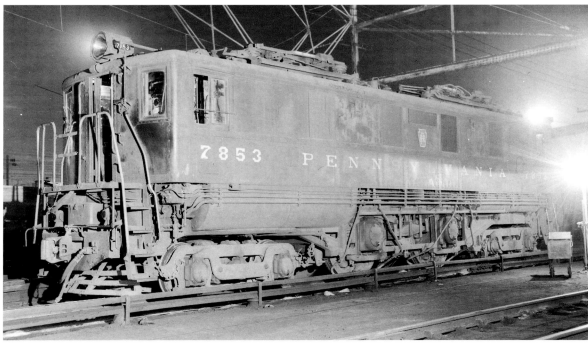

▸ GG1 4818 was almost obscured by a cloud of steam as a hostler at the Wilmington, Del., engine terminal cleaned road grime from the locomotive's trucks in 1960. Raymond S. Cole photo

▸▸A February 1960 view of the overhaul bay at the Pennsylvania's Wilmington shops found a lone modified P5a sharing space with ranks of GG1s. No. 4749 was one of the last of the aging P5a units to be overhauled as new General Electric E44s began to take the place of the older electrics. Don Wood photo

▶ At the south end of the New York-Washington electrification the Pennsylvania's electric fleet was serviced at the Washington Union Terminal's Ivy City engine terminal. Their inspection and servicing complete, GG1s 4874 and 4905 waited at Ivy City for their next assignment. One was still in the railroad's original pinstriped livery, while the other was finished in the newer style adopted in the mid-1950s. Jim Shaughnessy photo

◄ Readying a GG1 for another trip, a workman scrubbed the headlight at the Ivy City terminal. Jim Shaughnessy photo

▲ On a June night at Ivy City in 1960 GG1s received sand, fuel for their boilers, and a general inspection to ready them for another run. Jim Shaughnessy photo

► Waiting for servicing or their next run north over the Pennsylvania's busy New York-Washington main line, GG1s were lined up at Washington's Ivy City terminal in November 1967. William D. Middleton photo

◄ Enola Yard, across the Susquehanna River from Harrisburg, was the westernmost point reached by the Pennsylvania's electrification, and the engine terminal there was a major servicing and maintenance base for electric freight power. P5a boxcabs were inspected and filled with sand for their eastbound runs at the Enola sand tower on a November night in 1952. (both) Philip R. Hastings photo

▶ A train crew going off duty at the Enola engine terminal in November 1965 walked between ranks of the Pennsylvania's aging GG1s and the new E44s that were taking their place. The second unit in the row at left was prototype GG1 4800, the only one of the 139-unit fleet with a riveted, rather than welded, car body. Richard Steinheimer photo

▶▶A 1965 night scene at the Enola terminal reveals a variety of Pennsylvania motive power. At left are two EMD GP35 diesels. Several of the enduring GG1s are lined up on the tracks at the center, while an E44 is being serviced in the shop building to the right. Richard Steinheimer photo

The Ubiquitous MP54

For its initial Main Line suburban electrification of 1915 between Philadelphia and Paoli, the Pennsylvania put into service a fleet of 93 Class MP54 electric multiple-unit passenger cars. These were 64-foot-long, all-steel coaches originally built for steam-powered suburban service, but designed for later conversion to electric operation. A low monitor roof provided ample room to mount a pantograph, and a pair of porthole windows in each end gave the cars a distinctive "owl-eye" appearance. Spartan interiors were fitted with upholstered straight-back, walkover seats for 72 passengers. The railroad's Altoona shops equipped each car for electric service with a pantograph, a transformer to step down the 11,000-volt trolley wire voltage, and two 225-h.p. Westinghouse single-phase A.C. series traction motors, both mounted on the same truck. A control cab at each end was fitted with multiple-unit control equipment that provided automatic acceleration at a rate of 1 m.p.h. per second, and the cars had a balancing speed of 60 m.p.h.

As additional suburban lines

▶ No. 483 was typical of the hundreds of MP54 multiple-unit cars that fulfilled the lion's share of the Pennsylvania's electric commuter schedules for more than a half century. One of the later MP54s built, No. 483 was fitted with roller bearings and had two 368-h.p. traction motors, which provided sufficient power to pull a trailer. The louvers in the side ventilated the car's transformer, which converted the 11,000-volt trolley wire current to 850 volts. Pennsylvania Railroad photo were converted to electric operation at Philadelphia and in the New York area, the MP54 fleet was expanded through additional conversions or the construction of new cars, and the distinctive cars remained the Pennsylvania's standard M.U. car for more than 40 years. Some were built by outside car building plants, but most of the MP54 fleet was built in the Pennsylvania's own Altoona shops. Most were coaches, but there were also combination passenger-baggage, baggage, and baggage-RPO versions. Altogether, the Pennsylvania's MP54 fleet reached a total of more than 500 cars.

Some later MP54s were fitted with a pair of more powerful 368-h.p. traction motors and operated semipermanently coupled with nonpowered trailers. A few MP54s were later experimentally equipped with air-conditioning, and in 1949 one car was tested with experimental ignitron-rectifier tubes and D.C. traction motors. In 1950 the Pennsylvania began an MP54 rebuild program at its Wilmington shops that saw 99 cars equipped with new equalized trucks and roller bearings, aluminum window sash, and upgraded interiors. Less than a decade later, however, the Penn-

sylvania acquired the first of its modern stainless steel M.U. cars, and the days of the MP54 were numbered.

The Pennsylvania's two electrified subsidiaries both operated third-rail D.C. versions of the sturdy MP54 as well. In 1912 the West Jersey & Seashore augmented its original fleet of wooden M.U. cars with a batch of 17 steel MP54s, while the Long Island Rail Road operated an MP54 fleet in its heavy New York commuter service that was even larger than that of the parent PRR. The Long Island

acquired its first MP54s even before the Pennsylvania, when American Car & Foundry built 222 of them during 1909-10 for the railroad's new Penn Station service, and the LIRR MP54 fleet reached a total of close to a thousand cars by 1930. Aside from being equipped for third-rail D.C. operation, the earliest Long Island cars were almost identical to the Pennsylvania's MP54s, but later versions were built with a high-arch roof that gave them a distinctively different LIRR appearance.

▲ In a typical scene of Pennsylvania mainline multiple-unit activity, a four-car train of MP54s paused at Elizabeth in May 1966. The lead car was one of a number of MP54s modernized at the railroad's Wilmington shops during 1950-53 with new electrical equipment, roller bearing trucks, updated interiors, and other improvements. Some, including this car, got new doors and aluminum window sash. Robert J. Yanosey photo

The Pennsylvania's Electric Locomotives

Operation of the Pennsylvania's unprecedented electrification required an entirely new fleet of electric locomotives, and in characteristic PRR fashion the railroad set out to develop and test its own designs.

The railroad had already developed a satisfactory electric switching locomotive. A half dozen Class BB2 switchers built for the New York and Philadelphia terminal electrifications in 1926 were made up of paired 0-C-0 units. Another 14 individual Class B1 0-C-0 switchers were built at Altoona for the expanding A.C. electrification in 1934, while the original pairs were separated and reclassified as B1s.

It had already been determined that the L5 "Universal" design of 1924-28 would not be satisfactory for high-speed mainline electrification, and the railroad's motive power department developed standardized designs for three new boxcab electric locomotives. Class O1 was a 2-B-2 light passenger

unit, while Class P5 was a 2-C-2 unit designed for heavy passenger service. Class L6 was a 1-D-1 freight locomotive.

This initial attempt at developing a family of electric locomotives was anything but a success. The first of the standardized units to enter service were eight of the O1 units completed at Altoona in 1930 and 1931. The O1 proved to be too light for versatile passenger use, and experienced some tracking problems as well, and the design was never repeated. Only three prototype L6 freight locomotives ever entered service, while another 29 completed by the Lima Locomotive Works in 1934 were never fitted with electrical equipment and were finally scrapped without ever having pulled a train.

The L6 debacle was due not to any fault with their design, but rather to a series of misfortunes in the development of the standardized P5 heavy passenger units. Even before two prototype P5s had been completed at Altoona in

1931, the Pennsylvania had placed orders with Baldwin-Westinghouse, General Electric, and its own Altoona shops for an additional 90 improved P5a's. Intended to be the principal passenger motive power for the electrified lines, these powerful, 90-m.p.h. units were delivered during 1932-35.

The P5a's began handling through passenger trains in 1933, and it was not long before some serious shortcomings in their design began to appear. The unsuitability of the boxcab design for high-speed service was made clear by a January 1934 grade crossing collision at Deans, N.J., that claimed the life of an engineman. This was resolved by a redesign of the last 28 P5a units to a streamlined center-cab arrangement that afforded better protection for the engine crew. Other problems that began to show themselves soon after the locomotives entered service were not so easily corrected. While the P5a

◄ The Pennsylvania got its first standard A.C. electric locomotive in 1926 with the development of the BB2 class switcher, each of which was made up of paired O-C-O units. These were later separated and operated as individual B1 class units like No. 3921, seen here at New York's Sunnyside Yard in 1960. The switchers were built at the railroad's Altoona shops and were equipped with Westinghouse electrical components. Jim Shaughnessy photo

▶ The first of the railroad's new standard A.C. road locomotives to take the rails were these Class O1 passenger units, eight of which were completed at Altoona during 1930-31. No. 7850, the first one completed in July 1930, was one of three equipped with Westinghouse electrical equipment, while others were fitted with General Electric and Brown Boveri apparatus. Although they were not particularly successful, and no further examples were ever built, a few O1s remained in service for 30 years. David P. Morgan Library photo

▶ Complete except for the installation of electrical equipment and painting, a boxcab P5a unit stood on the erecting floor of the Baldwin Locomotive Works. Baldwin built 54 of the 2-C-2 P5a's between 1932 and 1935, while General Electric built another 25. The balance of the Pennsylvania's 92-unit P5 fleet was built at its own Altoona shops. Westinghouse or GE supplied electrical equipment for the entire fleet. H. L. Broadbelt Collection

high torque of more than 2000 h.p. on each axle. In the fall of 1933 the locomotives were withdrawn from service and steam power was restored to the main line while the P5 fleet was sent to the railroad's Wilmington shops for suspension modifications and new, heavier axles. Even with these changes it was clear that the P5a would not allow the Pennsylvania to gain the full level of performance that was possible from electrification. A new electric passenger locomotive design would be needed. Ultimately, the P5a fleet would be regeared for freight service, and the planned L6 freight locomotive program would be terminated.

The P5a's tracking problems had been analyzed on a special high-speed test track set up on the main line near Claymont, Del., in

proved powerful enough to pull trains of eight to ten cars, double-heading was required to maintain schedules. Serious tracking problems were encountered at high speeds, and the Pennsylvania was obliged to limit the P5a to 70 m.p.h. and to defer a planned acceleration of its passenger schedules in electrified territory. Cracks began to develop in the P5a driving axles from the extremely

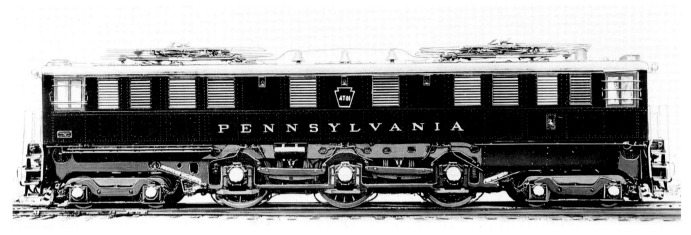

1933, with impact-recording ties and locomotive-mounted recording equipment to measure lateral forces against axles and wheel flanges. A continuing series of tests on this test track during 1933-34 was aimed at developing an electric locomotive with better riding qualities.

The first tests were conducted with a New Haven Class EP-3a locomotive built by General Electric in 1931. Unlike the Pennsylvania's standardized designs, which concentrated maximum weight and horsepower on each axle, the EP-3a spread an equivalent weight and horsepower over a greater number of axles. And unlike the rigid frame designs typical of PRR practice, the EP-3a employed an articulated frame, with a 2-C+C-2 wheel arrangement.

Tested at a maximum speed of 120 m.p.h., the New Haven unit showed superior tracking qualities and impact on the track structure less than that of the Pennsylvania's modified P5a design.

Much impressed by these results, the Pennsylvania promptly ordered a prototype Class GG1 locomotive from the Baldwin Locomotive Works, with electrical equipment from General Electric. Delivered in September 1934, GG1 4899 (later renumbered 4800 when series production began) was carried on two articulated cast-steel frames, with the same 2-C+C-2 wheel arrangement as the New Haven's EP-3a. The GG1 was 79 feet 6 inches long between coupler faces and weighed 230 tons. Its streamlined car body, with a sort of long-hooded steeple-cab

arrangement, was similar to that of the modified P5a units. A dozen A.C. traction motors gave the GG1 a continuous rating of 4620 h.p. at a maximum speed of 100 m.p.h., and it was capable of a short-term output of 8500 h.p.

During 1934 the prototype GG1 was tested at Claymont together with a prototype R1 unit built by Baldwin-Westinghouse that reflected a more typical PRR design approach, with a high-axle-load, rigid-frame, 2-D-2 wheel arrangement. The GG1 demonstrated tracking qualities that were much superior to those of the R1, and it imposed much lower lateral forces on the rail. In some tests, the GG1 reached a maximum speed of 115 m.p.h., and it proved capable of accelerating a test train from a stop to 100 m.p.h. in as little as 64.5

▲ No. 4701 was the very first production P5a completed by Baldwin in June 1932. Westinghouse supplied the electrical equipment. The massive boxcab front end, boxed headlight, keystone emblem, and horizontally barred pilot conveyed an unmistakable impression of Pennsylvania Railroad power. (both) H. L. Broadbelt Collection

▶ A 1934 grade crossing accident that took the life of an engineman revealed the unsuitability of the P5a's boxcab design for high-speed operation, and the last 28 units were built to a modified streamlined center-cab arrangement that afforded better crew protection. The streamlined cab for one of these modified P5a's took shape on the floor of the Baldwin works in 1935. H. L. Broadbelt Collection

seconds. The following year prototype GG1 4800 reportedly reached a speed of 129 m.p.h. during a series of braking tests.

The Pennsylvania had found a locomotive to match its great electrification.

Orders were soon placed with General Electric and the Altoona shops for another 57 GG1s, all of which were delivered by August 1935. There were only minor differences between the prototype and production GG1s, the most visible reflecting the contributions of industrial designer Raymond Loewy, who suggested the use of a smooth, arc-welded body in place of the awkward riveted body of the

prototype and other refinements. The GG1s were finished in a dark—almost black—Brunswick green with five gold pinstripes along the flanks, creating an enduring image for what was to become the most celebrated electric locomotive ever built.

Still more orders followed, and by 1943 the GG1 fleet had reached a total of 139 locomotives. For close to 40 years the GG1 reigned supreme over the Pennsylvania's great eastern electrification. It was the GG1, together with the great capacity inherent in the railroad's heavy-duty electrification, that made possible the Pennsylvania's extraordinary performance of the

World War II years. By 1959, when prototype GG1 4800 had been in service for 25 years, the Pennsylvania's GG1 fleet had accumulated a total of 337 million locomotive miles, equivalent to an average of more than 97 times around the world at the equator for each of the 139 locomotives in the fleet.

The GG1 was unexcelled in high-speed operation. Donald M. Steffee's 1948 annual speed survey for *Railroad* magazine, for example, reported a daily total of more than 17,000 miles operated at mile-a-minute or better timings on the GG1-equipped Pennsylvania electrification. In his 1967 survey for *Trains*, Steffee noted that regeared GG1s were marking up an 85.5-m.p.h. start-to-stop average for the *Afternoon Congressional* between Baltimore and Wilmington that represented the fastest schedule anywhere in North America. And while they were best known as high-speed passenger locomotives, the GG1s regularly operated in fast, heavy freight service as well.

The Pennsylvania resumed its electric locomotive development program in the years following World War II, with the earliest objective being the eventual replacement of the now-aging P5a fleet. Following its successful trials with an MP54 M.U. car equipped with an ignitron-rectifier and a D.C. traction motor, the railroad ordered several prototype locomotives in 1951. A pair of Class E3 two-unit, 6000-h.p. locomotives supplied by Westinghouse employed ignitron-rectifiers to supply D.C. power to the traction motors. One pair of E3b units employed a B-B-B wheel arrangement, while the other pair of E3c units had a C-C arrangement. Three E2b locomotives built by General Electric, each made up of a pair of B-B units, employed the same type of A.C. commutator motors used on earlier Pennsylvania locomotives.

Both designs worked well, but the ignitron-rectifier type was particularly successful, and it was the technology chosen when the Pennsylvania was finally ready to replace the P5a fleet almost a decade later. In 1959 the railroad announced that it had negotiated a long-term lease contract with General Electric for a fleet of 66 Class E44 rectifier freight locomotives. These were 193-ton, C-C units configured in a hood arrangement similar to a diesel-electric road switcher. Equipped with a bank of 12 ignitron mercury-arc rectifiers

and six D.C. traction motors identical to those used in diesel-electrics, the powerful E44 had a continuous rating of 4400 h.p. and could develop a starting tractive effort of 89,000 pounds. E44 deliveries began in 1960 and continued through 1963. Near the end of deliveries six units were fitted with a new type of silicon-diode rectifier, which increased the rated output to 5000 h.p., and the entire fleet was later fitted with the newer rectifiers.

The Pennsylvania's new E44 fleet was an extraordinary success. An E44 proved capable of more than half again as much work per unit month as the P5a it replaced,

and an E44 could handle 20 percent more tonnage than either a P5a or a GG1. Worthy successors to the electrics they replaced, the E44s proved to be the Pennsylvania's last new electric locomotive design. Less than five years after the last E44 went into service, the railroad was merged into the new Penn Central Company.

▲ Modified P5a 4780 showed off her streamlined lines in a record photo taken shortly after the locomotive was completed at the Pennsylvania's Altoona shops in December 1934. Westinghouse supplied the electrical apparatus for the 6000-h.p. locomotive. David P. Morgan Library photo

▶ Disappointed with the performance of its P5a fleet in fast passenger service, the Pennsylvania began an extensive series of tests and developed two new designs for evaluation. No. 4899 was a prototype 2-C+C-2 articulated GG1 unit completed by Baldwin in 1934, with GE electrical equipment. This view of the completed unit before the installation of electrical equipment and painting shows the GG1's streamlined center-cab arrangement, similar to that adopted at about the same time for the modified P5a design. (both) H. L. Broadbelt Collection

◀ The completed GG1 prototype, assigned road number 4899, looked like this. After the design was selected for series production, the unit would get a new road number—4800—and a handsome new pinstriped paint scheme developed by industrial designer Raymond Loewy. H. L. Broadbelt Collection

◀ Tested against the first GG1 was prototype Class R1 2-D-2 unit 4800, built by Baldwin, with Westinghouse electrical equipment. When the GG1 was selected for series production, the two prototypes exchanged road numbers. As the GG1 fleet grew, the R1 was renumbered again, to 4999. The R1 served out a long career as a one-of-a-kind unit. H. L. Broadbelt Collection

▶ GG1 prototype 4899 was readied for testing on the Pennsylvania's test track installation at Claymont. Special electromagnetic strain gauges and weigh bars applied to the ends of the axles measured lateral forces developed by the locomotive. Frederick Westing Collection

▶ No. 4899 is seen here during the Claymont tests on the main line between Philadelphia and Wilmington. In several tests the GG1 and its test car accelerated to 100 m.p.h. in just 64.5 seconds, and it reached a maximum speed of 115 m.p.h. with passenger trains. Frederick Westing Collection

▶▶ Renumbered 4800 but not yet repainted into the new Loewy design, the prototype GG1 was posed with 4-6-2 Pacific 5426, one of the Pennsylvania's celebrated K4 class, at Philadelphia on November 30, 1934. General Electric photo

▶ The sturdy steel frame of a GG1 looked like this before the welded steel skin was applied. This was one of the first 14 production GG1s built at General Electric's Erie plant in 1935. General Electric photo

▶ The GG1's distinctive streamlined design took shape as the steel skin was welded into place at GE's Erie plant. The use of a welded body shell in place of the riveted design of the prototype GG1 was one of the most visible of the design improvements recommended by designer Raymond Loewy. General Electric photo

◀ An engineman had this view ahead from the cab of a GG1. Visible through the cab window is one of the Pennsylvania's distinctive position light signals, while to the enginemen's left are the cab signal indicator and some of the many gauges and meters required for the operation of an electric locomotive. Pennsylvania Railroad photo

◀ This was the first production GG1, photographed shortly after its completion at GE's Erie works in May 1935. All of the design modifications proposed by Loewy — smoothly welded streamlined body, pinstriped paint scheme, and other detail refinements — are in place to create one of the most famous American locomotive designs of all time. General Electric photo

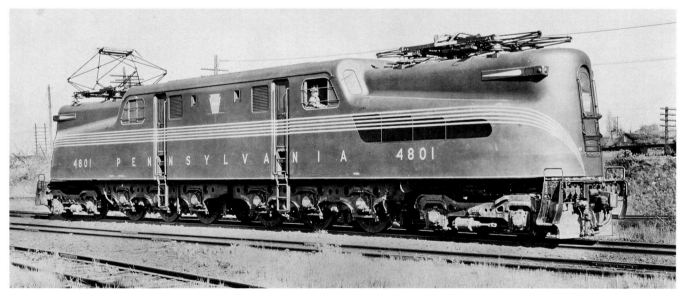

▶ Four of the most famous electric locomotives ever built were lined up for this memorable portrait of GG1s at rest by noted photographer O. Winston Link in October 1951. Pennsylvania Railroad photo

◀ ▲ In the late 1950s the GG1 fleet began to get an updated version of their classic Raymond Loewy styling. A single broad yellow band replaced the five gold pinstripes of the original design, the railroad name and road numbers were applied in oversized lettering, and a big red keystone emblem was applied to each side. GG1 4811 was just out of the paint shop at the railroad's Wilmington shops on February 27, 1960. (both) Don Wood photo

▶ There were occasional variations from the Pennsylvania's standard liveries for the GG1. Several members of the fleet appeared in the railroad's trademark tuscan red instead of the usual almost black Brunswick green. A more extreme variation was this aluminum-and-red scheme seen on GG1 4880 at Sunnyside Yard in 1955. James G. La Vake photo

◄ ▲ The Pennsylvania's post-
World War II electric locomotive
development included prototype
units from both General Electric and
Westinghouse. GE delivered three of
these Class E2b locomotives, each
made up of two B-B units powered
by A.C. commutator motors. Several
of the units were demonstrated on
the New Haven and Great Northern
electrifications before entering regular service on the Pennsylvania. Unit
4943 headed the railroad's eastbound symbol freight EC-5 at
Severn, Md., in September 1953.
(both) H. N. Proctor photo

▶ The Westinghouse contribution to the Pennsylvania's development program included a pair of two-unit, 6000-h.p. ignitron-rectifier locomotives, each with a different wheel arrangement. Shown here are E3b units 4995 and 4996, which had a B-B-B configuration. Westinghouse Electric & Manufacturing Co photo

▶ The second Westinghouse ignitron locomotive design was the E3c, made up of two of these C-C units. The new ignitron-rectifier technology incorporated in the Westinghouse units proved the most promising and formed the basis for the Pennsylvania's next big — and last — electric locomotive order. Westinghouse Electric & Manufacturing Co photo

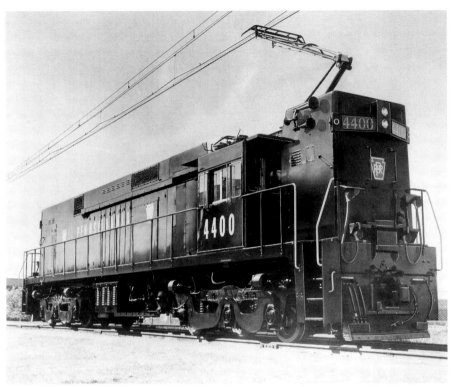

▲ If they lacked the aesthetics of earlier Pennsylvania electrics, the railroad's fleet of 66 Class E44 igni-tron-rectifier locomotives proved to be exceptionally capable performers. General Electric delivered the fleet over a three-year period from 1960 to 1963 under a long-term lease contract. No. 4400 was the first unit off the builder's Erie production line in late 1960. General Electric photo

▶ Configured in a boxy hood arrangement similar to diesel-electric road switchers and painted an unembellished dark green, the E44s were utilitarian in the extreme. Their one touch of glamour, the incorporation of cast bronze bells from retired steam locomotives, could be heard but not seen. Don Wood photo

What Might Have Been

▸ The Pennsylvania's Altoona shops turned out this 76½-foot, 240-ton monster in 1917 as a prototype for contemplated electrification across the Alleghenies. Billed as the "world's most powerful electric locomotive," the Class FF1 1-C+C-1 unit had four Westinghouse three-phase induction motors that produced a total hourly rating of 4800 h.p. and a maximum starting tractive effort of 140,000 pounds. Mountain electrification never came, and the big locomotive spent nearly 23 years in pusher service west of Philadelphia. David P. Morgan Library photo

Although it was to prove the high-water mark of Pennsylvania Railroad electrification, the extension of catenary westward to Harrisburg and Enola Yard that opened in 1938 was long seen as only a temporary stopping point for what was expected to be an even greater electrification across the Alleghenies to Pittsburgh.

The idea of electrification as a solution to the railroad's capacity limitations and operating problems on the difficult route across the Alleghenies had been around since at least 1908, when the Pennsylvania had initiated the first of many studies of the potential costs and benefits of electric traction. Although electrification looked promising, the uncertainties that attended the still-new technology caused the railroad to hesitate, and the work was put off. In 1913 the Pennsylvania's annual report told stockholders that a more modest electrification was being considered that would involve only about 35 miles of line over the Alleghenies between Altoona and Conemaugh. This time the work was deferred until earnings improved.

The subject of electrification west of Harrisburg was revisited often over the next four decades. In 1917 there was enough interest in a prospective electrification over the mountains for the railroad to build a prototype locomotive for test operation on the Paoli line electrification. Built at the Altoona shops with Westinghouse electrical equipment, this was the enormous, 240-ton Class FF1, a 4800-h.p., 1-C+C-1, single-phase A.C. unit that was billed as the "world's most powerful electric locomotive." Still the Pennsylvania held back from mountain electrification, and the FF1 served out her years as a pusher on the westbound grade between Overbrook, Pa., and Paoli.

Late in 1923 there were reports from the railroad's Philadelphia headquarters that electrification between Altoona and Conemaugh was imminent. Just a year later a

▸▸ The Pennsylvania was still thinking about electrification across the Alleghenies when L5 class 1-D-1 electric No. 3930 went into trial freight operation on the railroad's A.C. electrification west of Philadelphia in 1924. Built by the Altoona shops, with Westinghouse electrical equipment, it was the only one of the Pennsylvania's L5 class "Universal" A.C./D.C. locomotives actually equipped for A.C. operation. Although the design failed to live up to expectations, No. 3930 remained in service for 20 years. Chaney Collection, Smithsonian Institution (Neg. 10366)

second test unit for future heavy mainline electrification, the only single-phase A.C. version of the railroad's Class L5 1-D-1 "Universal" locomotive, was turned out by the Altoona shops. The railroad's priority soon shifted to electrification of its eastern main lines, but the idea of electrifying the Pennsylvania's high-density route across the Alleghenies was not forgotten. In 1930 it was reported that the Pennsylvania was preparing plans for electrifying its Middle and Pittsburgh divisions all the way to Pittsburgh. But with the enormous commitment of resources required for the Pennsylvania's eastern lines electrification, as well as the sharp decline of traffic and earnings that followed the great national depression, a mountain electrification was again deferred.

By 1936 the railroad was once again ready to consider the long-deferred project, and new studies of Middle and Pittsburgh division electrification were initiated. Altoona shops turned out still another prototype locomotive for prospective mountain electrification, the 5000-h.p., 2-B+B-2 Class DD2, in 1938. Yet another study was completed in 1941, but the U.S. entry into World War II soon intervened to bring any thought of further expansion of the railroad's electrification to a halt, at least until war's end.

Even before the end of the war, however, the Pennsylvania began updating its studies, while Westinghouse and General Electric began developing designs for new electric locomotives for the long-planned Harrisburg-Pittsburgh

electrification. Once again, however, the time was not right for such an enormous expenditure. At war's end, the Pennsylvania faced an enormous burden of deferred maintenance from the intense traffic of the wartime years, while its earnings were down. Within only a few more years the railroad had decided that a system-wide conversion from steam to diesel-electric motive power was a better investment than stringing catenary across the Alleghenies. Never again did the Pennsylvania Railroad seriously consider what would have been the greatest mountain electrification ever seen in North America.

A Pennsy Electrification Postscript

The 1968 merger of the Pennsylvania Railroad and the New York Central into the new Penn Central Company began a period of major change for the great electrification that the Pennsylvania had developed over the preceding half century.

New operators and changed conditions ultimately brought an end to electric freight operations on the former Pennsylvania lines, but for a time an expansion of electrified freight operations even appeared possible. In 1971, for example, the new Penn Central studied an extension of the former PRR electrification north to Selkirk Yard at Albany, N.Y., over the former New York Central line on the west shore of the Hudson River. And in 1975 and 1976 Penn Central began testing prototype 6000- and 10,000-h.p. electrics built by Electro-Motive under license from Sweden's ASEA. Penn Central's 1970 bankruptcy, however, precluded any real likelihood of major Penn Central investment in new electrification.

The new Conrail system, which emerged in 1976 from the wreckage of the Penn Central and other eastern bankruptcies, briefly considered an expansion of electrification as well. A 1979 study considered—once again—electric operation of the former Pennsylvania main line across the Alleghenies to Conway Yard at Pittsburgh, as well as an upgrade of the existing former PRR electrification and a new electrification over a former Reading-Central of New Jersey route between Philadelphia and northern New Jersey. But within less than two years Conrail had decided against either any new electrification or even continuation of the existing electrification, and electric freight operation over the former Pennsylvania system came to an abrupt end in 1981.

Electrified commuter services on the former Pennsylvania lines in northern New Jersey, at Philadelphia, and in the Baltimore-Washington area fared much

◄ The Metroliner high-speed train program initiated by the Pennsylvania in the mid-1960s continued under the new Penn Central Company, and the trains finally entered regular service in January 1969. Southbound New York-Washington Metroliner 2005 flashed through Lanham, Md., in October 1969. William D. Middleton photo

After May 1971 Amtrak took over the Metroliner high-speed program. Amtrak's northbound Washington-New York Metroliner 112 sped past the Landover, Md., substation in October 1979. William D. Middleton photo

better under the new order, as public support became available for major rehabilitation and modernization. In northern New Jersey public funding even provided an extension of catenary over 21 miles of the former PRR New York & Long Branch line, from South Amboy to Long Branch.

For intercity passenger service the changes were the most positive of all, as the Pennsylvania's electrification became the foundation for what would develop over the next several decades as North America's only true high-speed railroad. The groundwork for high speed had been laid in the high standards of the original electrification itself, the upgrade of track and other facilities that had accompanied it, and—finally—in the high-speed Metroliner program

the Pennsylvania had launched in the mid-1960s.

The troubled Metroliners were still not ready to go when the program passed to the new Penn Central Company early in 1968. Penn Central persevered in the effort to correct the train's performance and reliability problems, and in January 1969 the trains finally entered regular service. Although they never fully reached their original performance objectives, the Metroliners established a new standard for high-speed service in the New York-Washington corridor. Under one briefly operated early nonstop schedule, the train covered the 226-mile New York-Washington run in just 2 hours 30 minutes, fully 50 minutes faster than the best schedule ever operated with a GG1 locomotive. By

the end of 1969 Penn Central was operating six daily Metroliner round trips, and by May 1972 Amtrak, which had taken over intercity passenger operations from Penn Central in 1971, was operating 14 daily Metroliner round trips. Most important, a long decline in passenger traffic in the corridor had been reversed.

Equally important to the future of high-speed service was a massive upgrade of fixed plant in what was now being called the Northeast Corridor. The original program begun in 1965 had included a substantial mileage of new continuous welded rail, re-ballasting, and resurfacing to permit the planned higher speeds. Several years later this was followed by the federally funded Northeast Corridor Improvement Program, which

▶ The last stand for the troubled Metroliners came during the 1980s in Philadelphia-Harrisburg service. Three-car Metroliner train 605 raced westward through Elizabethtown, Pa., en route to Harrisburg in April 1984. William D. Middleton photo

provided a massive upgrade of the entire 226-mile corridor, with a goal of 120-m.p.h. operation. By the time the $2.5 billion program was substantially complete in the mid-1980s, the entire corridor had been rebuilt with continuous welded rail and concrete ties, and a number of curves had been realigned. Bridges and tunnels had been rehabilitated, and the last grade crossings in the corridor had been eliminated. Train control and signaling were improved, and interlocking plants had been rehabilitated or reconfigured.

Even before the physical upgrade of the corridor was well started, Amtrak had begun a search for a new generation of electric motive power that could replace the aging GG1 fleet and meet the ambitious speed objec-

tives of the upgraded corridor. Faced with continuing problems with the Metroliner M.U. fleet, Amtrak decided on a more conventional locomotive-hauled approach for a new high-speed train program.

The passenger railroad's first venture in new electric motive power proved disappointing. In 1972 Amtrak ordered 26 6000-h.p., 120-m.p.h. E60 locomotives from General Electric that were a high-speed passenger version of a thyristor-rectifier freight locomotive developed for a new Arizona coal line. High-speed tracking problems, however, prevented the E60s from ever reaching their maximum speed objective. Some of the big C-C electrics were sold and the balance were limited to 90 m.p.h. on heavy through trains in

the corridor, while Amtrak resumed its search for a new high-speed locomotive.

As part of a renewed effort at finding a suitable new locomotive, Amtrak leased and tested a Swedish State Railways 6000-h.p. ASEA Rc4 unit and a French National Railways 7725-h.p. Alsthom-Atlantique unit during 1976–77. The Swedish electric proved to be just what Amtrak was looking for, and by the end of 1977 the railroad had ordered the first eight units of an AEM7 fleet that would eventually reach a total of 52 locomotives. Built by GM's Electro-Motive Division under license from ASEA, the AEM7 was a 5800-h.p., 125-m.p.h. version of the Swedish builder's lightweight B-B design, which had been built by the hundreds for European

systems. As the new electrics began to come on line, the troubled Metroliner M.U.s were gradually withdrawn from corridor service and replaced with AEM7-powered Amfleet Metroliners. With the new locomotives in service and the bulk of corridor rehabilitation complete, Amtrak was able to significantly accelerate its best New York-Washington timings. Within a few years virtually all Metroliner trains were operating over the 226-mile route in less than 3 hours, and by 1991 nonstop Express Metroliners were making the run in as little as 2 hours, 30 minutes.

Speeds over the former Pennsylvania electrification were notched up again under the federally funded Northeast High Speed Rail Improvement Program of the 1990s, which included both New Haven-Boston electrification and track upgrade in the northern end of the corridor and a new fleet of high-speed trainsets and locomotives. As a preliminary to developing specifications for this new generation of trains, Amtrak in 1993 began tests of both a Swedish-built X2000 high-speed tilting train and a German ICE train in corridor Metroliner service. Early in 1996 a Bombardier/GEC Alsthom team landed a contract for a new fleet of 20 high-speed Acela Express trainsets that would be capable of a maximum speed of 165 m.p.h. Each eight-car trainset included two power cars with a combined power output of 12,500 h.p., and incorporated a tilting mechanism that allowed higher speeds on curves without passenger discomfort. Also included in the order were 15 HHP-8 locomotives rated at 8000 h.p. and capable of a 150-m.p.h. maximum speed that would be employed on other corridor trains.

This new generation of electrics began to enter regular service near the end of 2000, bringing fastest-ever timings to the New York-Washington route. As the twenty-first century began, the great high-speed corridor created by the Pennsylvania Railroad's massive electrification program of the 1930s still reigned as North America's premier high-speed passenger rail corridor, as it had for most of the twentieth century.

◀ A fleet of 26 of these 6000-h.p. E60 locomotives built for Amtrak by General Electric during 1974-75 was intended as replacements for the aging GG1s, but tracking problems prevented the big locomotives from ever operating at their intended 120-m.p.h. maximum. No. 973 headed train 174, the northbound *Statesman-Connecticut Yankee*, through Lanham on February 12, 1977. Fred W. Schneider III photo

◄◄ Minutes out of New York's Penn Station, an E60 with a southbound Northeast Corridor train emerged from the Passaic River lift bridge into Newark's Penn Station in May 1995. William D. Middleton photo

◄ A leased Swedish-built ASEA Rc4 electric proved to be the high-speed locomotive Amtrak was looking for, and General Motors' Electro-Motive Division ultimately built 52 5800-h.p., 125-m.p.h. AEM7 versions of the speedy boxcab units for Amtrak. One of them flashed through Glenn Dale, Md., with a northbound Metroliner in August 1981. William D. Middleton photo

◄◄ AEM7 935 raced up the corridor's center track near the Delaware Park Race Track west of Wilmington on May 7, 1988, with northbound Washington-New York train 140, the *Potomac*. William D. Middleton photo

◄ Another new era of high-speed operation built on the foundation of the Pennsylvania Railroad's great electrification began in November 2000. Acela Express train set 5 entered New York's Pennsylvania Station on a November 16 pre-inaugural run from Washington to Boston. Regular service with the new trains began on December 11, 2000. Joseph M. Calisi photo

Recommended Reading

Bezilla, Michael, *Electric Traction on the Pennsylvania Railroad, 1895–1968*. University Park, Pa., The Pennsylvania State University Press, 1980.

Burgess, George H., and Miles C. Kennedy, *Centennial History of the Pennsylvania Railroad Company: 1846–1946*. Philadelphia, Pennsylvania Railroad Company, 1949.

Middleton, William D., *Manhattan Gateway*. Waukesha, Wis., Kalmbach Books, 1996.

————— , *When the Steam Railroads Electrified*. Revised second edition. Bloomington, Ind., Indiana University Press, 2001.

Staufer, Alvin F., *Pennsy Power: Steam and Electric Locomotives of the Pennsylvania Railroad, 1900–1957*. Medina, Ohio, Alvin F. Staufer, 1962.

————— , and Bert Pennypacker, *Pennsy Power II: Steam, Diesel and Electric Locomotives of the Pennsylvania Railroad*. Medina, Ohio, Alvin F. Staufer, 1968.

Index of Photographs

Photographers